LEADERSHIP

PANDORA'S BOX

by LINKED IN AND TOWN HALL ACHIEVER OF THE YEAR

EY NOMINEE ENTREPRENEUR OF THE YEAR

GRAND HOMAGE LYS DIVERSITY

Dr. BAK NGUYEN, DMD

TO ALL OF US, CITIZEN, COUNTRYMEN AND WOMAN, TO
NEVER FEEL LEFT OUT AND WITHOUT A VOICE. THERE IS
ALWAYS HOPE.

by Dr. BAK NGUYEN

ISBN: 978-1-989536-19-3

LEADERSHIP
PANDORA'S BOX
by Dr. BAK NGUYEN

INTRODUCTION
BY Dr. BAK NGUYEN

HOPE
CHAPTER 1
THE POWER OF HOPE

SELF AWARENESS
CHAPTER 2
AN ODE TO AWARENESS

LOYALTY
CHAPTER 3
THE BLOODLINES OF LOYALTY

CONCLUSION
THE TRAIN OF LIFE
BY Dr. BAK NGUYEN

Introduction
by Dr. Bak Nguyen

It's been less than two weeks since the last chapter of **SYMPHONY OF SKILLS**. I thought that it would take me some time before I start writing something new. Once again, I was wrong.

Since it's now the end of October and the pool is closed until next May, I have to do something with the **Momentum** from **SYMPHONY OF SKILLS**. The 20 laps energy will have to go on, so what's next?

I did enjoy writing and learning about you, life, and myself. Most people felt in love with **SYMPHONY OF SKILLS**. Many were wondering when I will write again, but this time to all, not just to entrepreneurs.

Each time, I smiled, not knowing what to respond. In the meantime, I got involved in helping a friend of mine running for mayor. I applied some of the **SYMPHONY OF SKILLS'** theories to politic, and suddenly, everything became simple and clear!

I got caught in the charm and dove into some of the famous political speeches of presidents and influencers in modern times. Speeches from President John F. Kennedy, from president Barack Obama, from Mohamed Ali, from admiral William McRaven and, of course, Steve Jobs.

That's power, words that can lift the spirit and the world with it! You cannot stay immune to the words of those great men. It makes sense, it sounds right, and yet, they are talking about things that aren't however!

Then, I discovered an elite group of philosophers names Fearless Motivation. After two weeks of listening to all those great minds, I couldn't resist anymore.

Life and creativity come from the interaction of two strong opposites.
Dr. Bak Nguyen

I firmly believe that **LEADERSHIP, PANDORA'S BOX**, will benefit much from, not just my thoughts and creativity but from the life resulting from the clashes of our minds.

This book will be about the next installments of **ENTREPRENEURSHIP, SYMPHONY OF SKILLS**, about how we should apply the powers of the entrepreneur into our world, for the greater good! The first title was:

SOCIAL ENTREPRENEURSHIP, Pandora's box.
- Dr. Bak Nguyen

But after the first chapter about Hope was written, it became clear that I have evolved since **ENTREPRENEURSHIP, SYMPHONY OF SKILLS**.

This is **LEADERSHIP**. I do not pretend that I know leadership, but I will tell you that **LEADERSHIP** is something that I can feel, clearly now.

I do not believe in compromise nor half-truth. I am a person that will take a stand and is not scared of a fight. More than that, I aspired to grow through this journey, to exchange with respect and learn from each other.

This endeavor will be more than a philosophical exercise. I aim to cover 21 different themes of leadership that could impact the world of tomorrow.

Yes, I want this book to matter and to inspire anyone of us, citizen of the world, to make a difference. Each of the chapters will comprise of a presidential speech like to inspire the next leaders among us. To do good.

Dear citizen of the world, my fellow entrepreneurs, I hope that you will all find the depth that you were looking for within these lines.

I hope that the emotional content and rise will strike those chords inside your heart, so your soul starts to sing along. This is not a one-person endeavor, the world needs all of us, and we owe it to ourself to give it our best!

Citizen of the world, entrepreneurs, **LionHearts**, I salute you!

OUR
FOCUS
TODAY
WILL
DEFINE
OUR MEAL
TOMORROW.

-DR. BAK NGUYEN

Chapter 1
"The Power of Hope"
Speech by Dr. Bak Nguyen

Hope is the Will within every single heart.
- Dr. Bak Nguyen

Hope is the **Will** within every single heart. The power of Hope comes from the fact that it is accessible to anyone and everyone. **Hope** is the light that keeps us from giving up. That pushes us a little more down the road until it gets a little easier.

Hope is what keeps our heart beating even when everything seems lost. It is now conventional wisdom that, there is no failure until one quits. As long as there is **Hope**, the quitting cannot occur.

Hope can take seed in any heart, as small and little as the heart is. It lives, grows, and replicates as if it touches another life. A simple touch, a dedicated look, a smile, **Hope** replicates itself in each of those mondaine interactions.

That is why **Hope** cannot be beaten nor killed. But much more, **Hope** is so powerful because it is highly contagious! Once spread, it cannot be stopped.

Hope then, grows into a storm, taking it seed from a single heart, a **LionHeart**. That **LionHeart** is the leader, the believer, the source of strength for change to happen.

With the **power of Hope**, the **LionHeart** embodies the **Will** of the people and will grow into a mountain with the breath of a dragon.

They will try to strike it down with fear, fear of change, fear of pain, fear of losing everything. But **Hope**, like fire, is resilient. The more fear is striking, like a strong wind, the more **Hope** is spreading, discreet, from one heart to the next.

Nothing can silence **Hope** but **complacency**. Just like fire without air, **Hope** then, cannot exist.

If you want to silence **Hope**, get people to believe that everything is all right, give them something to hold on to so that the fear of losing that comfort, as small as it is, keeps **complacency** in their hearts and minds.

With contentment, **Hope** cannot exist. **Hope** cannot grow. So be fearful and aware of what kind of comfort you trade in your freedom for. Because precisely like fire, to start one, it will take pain and sacrifice.

Often, it is said that the winners have to go the extra mile, that the achievers sacrifice everything, that they didn't hold anything back. It is possible because they believed they had **Hope**.

That's the power of Hope; it starts small and grows into a storm.
- Dr. Bak Nguyen

In those **LionHearts**, Hope has **grown** strong until it embodied the spirits themselves. **Hope** is now part of the DNA. It has become confidence and, in time, confidence will grow into the love of winning!

A winning heart does not need **Hope** anymore, and it knows that it will! It sees what will be.

Nowadays, in the depth of the information age, technology, and the internet have spread all around the world. Within it, the social networks have prospered and entered each of our houses, in both of our pockets.

We can discuss timelessly the pros and cons, but one thing is undeniable, for the first time in human history, we can take back the control.

Of course, the world is still lead by the elites and the governments. But they cannot strike pure fear to silence us anymore. Hope, through the web, is a tidal wave that no single force can resist.

So, if that is true, why are there still poverty, injustice, and suffering? Because of complacency. Because we don't care!

DIVIDE TO CONQUER

That's the real enemy of a better tomorrow, **complacency**. If we don't care, there is no more hope. If we don't care, we will die taking more from this world than we gave.

If we don't care, we will condemn our children to solve our problems. If we don't care, people are dying... and some we may even know.

Citizen of the world, we have a choice to make. We can talk about hope, about a better tomorrow, but for as long as we do not give up on our **complacency**, we won't matter. We are part of the problem.

Entrepreneurs, **LionHearts**, it is our responsibility to lead the way, to spread the fire of hope and the love for winning, for achieving. For our world to be a better one for our children, we need more than to hope, and we need to succeed!

We need a plan and the wisdom that we might fail. As long as **Hope** grows by our side, another will take over from where we failed, until we come back and double down on our effort.

Together, with the **power of Hope** igniting our hearts, we will elevate this world to new heights, heights our grandchildren will take for granted! Just as our forefathers have done before us.

The legacy is strong, and the **Hope** is powerful, our world will thrive!

Citizen of the world, entrepreneurs, **LionHearts**, I salute you!

LIFE

AND CREATIVITY

COME FROM THE

INTERACTION OF TWO

STRONG OPPOSITES.

-DR. BAK NGUYEN

Chapter 2
"An Ode to Awareness"
Speech by Dr. Bak Nguyen

One must know oneself, know other and then, and only then, one can go. Our journey started the moment we opened our eyes for the first time. We learn to breathe, to feel, to feed.

Then, we learn to smile, to walk, and to absorb our surroundings. From wish to knowledge, from certainty to projection, we try our best to live up to the task. All along, we've learned, we've grown.

The **quest of identity** is not a resting one since we are continually put to the test. When there is no exterior stress, we are self investigating. There is simply no rest.

More questions than answers emerge at each session. It's the purpose of the exercise, but it is also the biggest trap of the quest.

To try to answer all the questions correctly will push us digging further, in directions, we might not even care. The goal of the exercise was to be able to rise from the doubt and decide which questions define us and merit our attention.

Yes, the items we choose will define us. We will walk out of our **quest of identity** with a set of questions, not a set of answers.

The values we bear in our hearts are no certainty, and there are the quests we will embrace on our journey, to prove them right. Some will be proven wrong, and then, we will know, because we've walked the path.

Even so, we won't discard them at first sight of weakness. We will stand for our values and test them again, and again, trying to find another way.

That's the character, once we have decided on our values. Even those values proven right, won't be right all the time.

Sometimes, we will be tormented by the confusion between our beliefs and reality. Not every time, we will turn life into our reality. That's wisdom, once we've known who we are. We will choose what matters and when to move on.

Curiosity is the **consistency** in our quest to find answers to our values. Some of us will have chosen to gather and keep a more extensive set while others will pack as naturally as possible. It does not matter.

The merit is in the decision first to define our set of values. The journey will begin, those adventures and experiences, they are the ones that matter since they are the one forging our legend and our soul from the fire of life. Along the path, we will change. Of course, we will change, that was the intended point!

Each step we took, as long as it was from our own will, will lead us closer to empowerment, to self-fulfillment.

One's legend can only begin the day one's quest of identity is over.
- Dr. Bak Nguyen

To be able to walk the path, we must have defined our values first. Those values even as interrogations themselves with stirring us in the vastness of the canvas.

We will see many things, and we will taste colors and sounds unknown to us, we will feel love and fear both leaving scars on our heart. Every time, we will come up ahead, taking our breath from the horizon. One must know that all he'll see, taste and touch will change him.

False! With our values and beliefs, we are the one changing everything we've touched for better or for worst, and it's up to our values.

The colors, the tastes, the texture, we'll see everything through own perspective, through our glasses. It can't be otherwise. That is why it is so important to have defined ourselves before taking on the journey.

We will meet with people on the way, and we will define them by touching them. They will react to us and so will start a relationship, through our values, through our glasses.

What we like or hate in them are not what there are; it's what we see. Our relationship is their reaction upon what we've projected. And they too are as blind as we are, they will know a self-image of themselves that they either like or hate.

That the twist of our journey, all the way, we will see mirrors of ourselves. To grow, we will have to learn to go beyond the lies and deceptions to be able to connect with another soul.

So don't judge, since you'll be judging yourself!
- Dr. Bak Nguyen

When two bodies meet, there is a rise in energy. Tension or excitement, the transfer of power is the same, flowing freely from one frame to the next without resistance, leaving a trail of sensations.

We will describe the color and catalog them using our values. Always, with our values. That is why we cannot take on the path without a consistent set of values.

They are the reference until we have grown enough to learn to go on without them. That day, we will have accomplished our legend. We will have built healthy and wise.

Citizen of the world, entrepreneurs, **LionHearts**, wonders lie ahead, waiting for us to discover. What we'll need to taste and enjoy the amazing is to master our destiny, and it started by defining our values.

We have to get out of the quest of identity as soon as possible, and the fun lies ahead! But don't rush either, because our values will affect everything we will come in contact with.

In other words, our values will shape the world of tomorrow; it will color our legend and will stir us in the vastness of the universe.

The world is ours to design, make it a great one, a peaceful one, an abundant one, one in which every soul can have a chance to happiness and a right to freedom.

Citizen of the world, entrepreneurs, **LionHearts**, I salute you!

THE TASTE OF

ABUNDANCE

DEMANDS

THAT

ONE GIVES UP

THE CARROT.

-DR. BAK NGUYEN

Chapter 3
"The bloodlines of Loyalty."
Speech by Dr. Bak Nguyen

Loyalty is a value of **nobility** — **loyalty** to one's country, to one's king, to one's brother. From the nursing cradle, we have been exposed to the greatness of faithfulness.

We spend our lives looking for it and trying to live up to it. What society has failed to disclose is that loyalty can only be binding if one has to choose so.

Therefore, never confuse **gratitude** with **loyalty**. As we are born, we have enjoyed a passive ride with our parents in the driver's seat.

Then, a society with education and social pressures gave us options and knowledge than we swallowed, often with an objection, but most of the time, we consumed.

As much as it is our life, we are a beneficiary, a passive customer. It's not until that we are reborn that our personal story starts. In other words, the day we give birth to ourself, our spirit, our personality, that day, we can finally begin our story.

One's story can only begin when one's quest for identity is over.
- Dr. Bak Nguyen

Out of the **quest of identity**, we may choose to change only wholly or partially our received personality, and only the name will remain.

Sooner or later, we will come out of it, and the only difference will be the time that we have left to walk our story and make it into a great one, a legend.

This is what we've learned from the first tome, **ENTREPRENEURSHIP, SYMPHONY OF SKILLS**. Now that we are, we can start to make our own choice. Only that day, **loyalty** can begin to bloom.

Up to that point, we've been served lies about loyalty and responsibility. Neither commitment nor responsibility can make any sense until we've started to make our own choice. **Gratitude**, sure, but not **loyalty**.

As crucial as **gratitude** is for one's character, it has nothing to do with loyalty. What's the difference? The difference is that some will go to the end road, make the ultimate sacrifice out **loyalty**, not **gratitude**.

That's the **power of commitment**, the **power of belief** into a more significant cause than ourself. It is the most powerful among the values available to the leadership. How can we put it into good use? Did I mean our **loyalty**?

The first **loyalty** one should have is towards him/herself. It is called integrity, **loyalty** to one's values. The keywords here are **OWN VALUES**.

That's how democracy has proven the least imperfect system throughout human history. Because we choose. Did we? How many times did you vote?

Then, loyalty will apply to your surroundings, your friends. That's also why often, it is easier to get closer to our friends than our siblings. We didn't choose our siblings, but our friends, we did.

Don't twist my words here, we can want to be closed and share with our siblings, but again, we need to choose to do so, not merely out of habit or convenience.

Loyalty to one's country is **loyalty** to real estate, it is stupid and idiot as would say « Dr. House » (from the popular TV show). But he has a point!

Until one has started traveling the world, he did not choose yet. As he goes to different countries, he will see the colors, he will taste what the world has to offer.

That day, he can choose to love or not the land of his birth. The journey is literal, and one will have to travel to discover the options and make his/her choice.

After the three ramifications of loyalty, one has earned his stripes to become a citizen. He knows what his values are and how to improve on them. From that day, a **LionHeart** is born, waiting to awake in time of need.

There is nothing more significant than a citizen with a **LionHeart** to serve his/her country and cause. Entrepreneurs and warriors all know that the winner is the one who believes the hardest and the longest.

In other words, the winner is the one who did not give up! Empowered by **loyalty**, a citizen with a

LionHeart can lay down his life! If death itself does not scare him, what will?

Being fearless is one of the high power available to each one of us. To master the skill, one needs to detach himself from everything.

To make sure that every choice he makes is his own, at every single moment. His loyalty has strengthened his values throughout every step of the way. He is aware of each decision and each consequence.

He accepts them and moves forward, pressing all with what he is toward achieving the ultimate goal. In front of a power that high, only another **LionHeart** will have a chance to stop the storm that has started.

Citizen of the world, entrepreneurs, **LionHearts**, we all have the power within us to be great, to achieve things our minds would not dare conceived yesterday.

Serving love and dedication, **loyalty** is the supreme weapon to mass, making everything one puts his heart into. Commitment, in the right place, can free one from the grasp of fear, from the hook of greed, which is two of the most corrupt emotions known to human.

To be great, you must embrace yourself. To do good, you must be **loyal**, to you, to your choices, to your values. You have the opportunity, you are the power, the power to bring the chance much needed into our world!

We need you, your **loyalty**, your achievements.

Citizen of the world, entrepreneurs, **LionHearts**, I salute you!

DON'T STAND

IN THE

WAY OF A

LOYAL HEART

BECAUSE

THERE

IS NO

VICTORY

POSSIBLE

-DR. BAK NGUYEN

Chapter 4

"The taste of abundance demands that one gives up the carrot!"

Speech by Dr. Bak Nguyen

God is **abundant**. God is the only will that can give or take, and he always gives for as long as we know how to receive. Do we have to fight for what is ours?

Among us, yes. But most of the time, we are fighting over the same piece of bone while the real rewards lie blindly in front of our eyes! Do you see the carrot or the turkey?

To taste **abundance**, we have to be willing to look beyond the low hanging fruits. When we concentrate on what's closed and near, our mind tunnel vision on the target, and we lose the perception of the horizon, of the whole, of reality itself. It's a matter of focus.

Our focus today will define our meal tomorrow.
- Dr. Bak Nguyen

To receive, we need to ask first. We need to get over our pride and laziness. We will have to prepare ourselves for what is coming because it's wrapped in shapes and colors that we cannot foresee.

Often, to taste the prize of **abundance** given to us, we will have to put in the work to dig it up. To hunt the prized prey, we will need to be faster, stronger, smarter.

Not as a test, but because it is the only way that we could enjoy the meal. Fight for the carrot, and you'll be a carrot eater. Hunt for the elephant and you will become a lion.

We have to grow into a giant to enjoy the feast! Until then, our stomach wasn't ready to swallow such greatness. It's not free, and it's **abundant**.

Are we all lions? We could be, but we will need to choose so. We will need to overcome our habits and **complacency** to see beyond the carrot.

Fighting among brothers is not worth it! Why, because it's not more comfortable, it does not make us any stronger, just more vile and alone... and we will still stay hungry.

Go for the **elephants**, and we will need the help of our brothers to carry the feast home. As we learn to do so, we will receive more than we asked for: we will have to break the loneliness and selfishness of the carrot to discover the **abundance of life** and the **spirit of brotherhood**.

With a bigger heart, anything is possible. With the help of our brothers, nothing is too high. Having tasted a feast once, we will never get back to the carrot.

So, my brothers and sisters, I urge you to stop looking at the carrot and see what lies beyond.

The sooner you'll do it, the sooner you'll embrace life the way God meant it to be.

We have invented words like heroes, champions, winners to identify those of us who have taken the lion path. When looking at them, a part of us envy them, want to be them. Keep that feeling and join them!

Grow your heart away from jealousy, from the fight of the carrot and join the team of champions. They are waiting for you.

If you are willing to learn and to step up, you will be walking among lions. Because they need you, they know it because their success depends on your progress.

The taste of abundance demands that one gives up the carrot!
- Dr. Bak Nguyen

Today, more than any other time in history, it has become harder and harder to see the horizon. So many disguised carrots hang before us.

The orange vision is more than a trend, and it is our reality. It has become our ambition. That where the end will strike, in an orange death!

Raise your heart, arise from your knees, and look at the sun for a moment. Feel its warm and fuel your body with passion. You are more than a carrot eater! We deserve more than an orange life, an average life!

Learn the lesson of abundance, take the strength of a champion, and eat like a lion! Do it for you, do it for those you cherish, do it to join your brotherhood, do it to taste life, do it to honour your creator fully!

We owe it to God and to ourself to see the future and lead the way. Life is full of elephants. There is no place for hunger. Experience is great, and there is no more space for the small.

The small minds, the tiny hearts, the small carrots. Show the little ones how to grow, to join the lions. Give them a taste the feast, and they will stop seeing the carrot. But you can only do so if you have felt the feast yourself.

Citizen of the world, entrepreneurs, **LionHearts**, our world can be abundant if you think so, hunger can be no more if you say so, war among brothers will cease if you choose so.

Citizen of the world, entrepreneurs, **LionHearts**, I salute you!

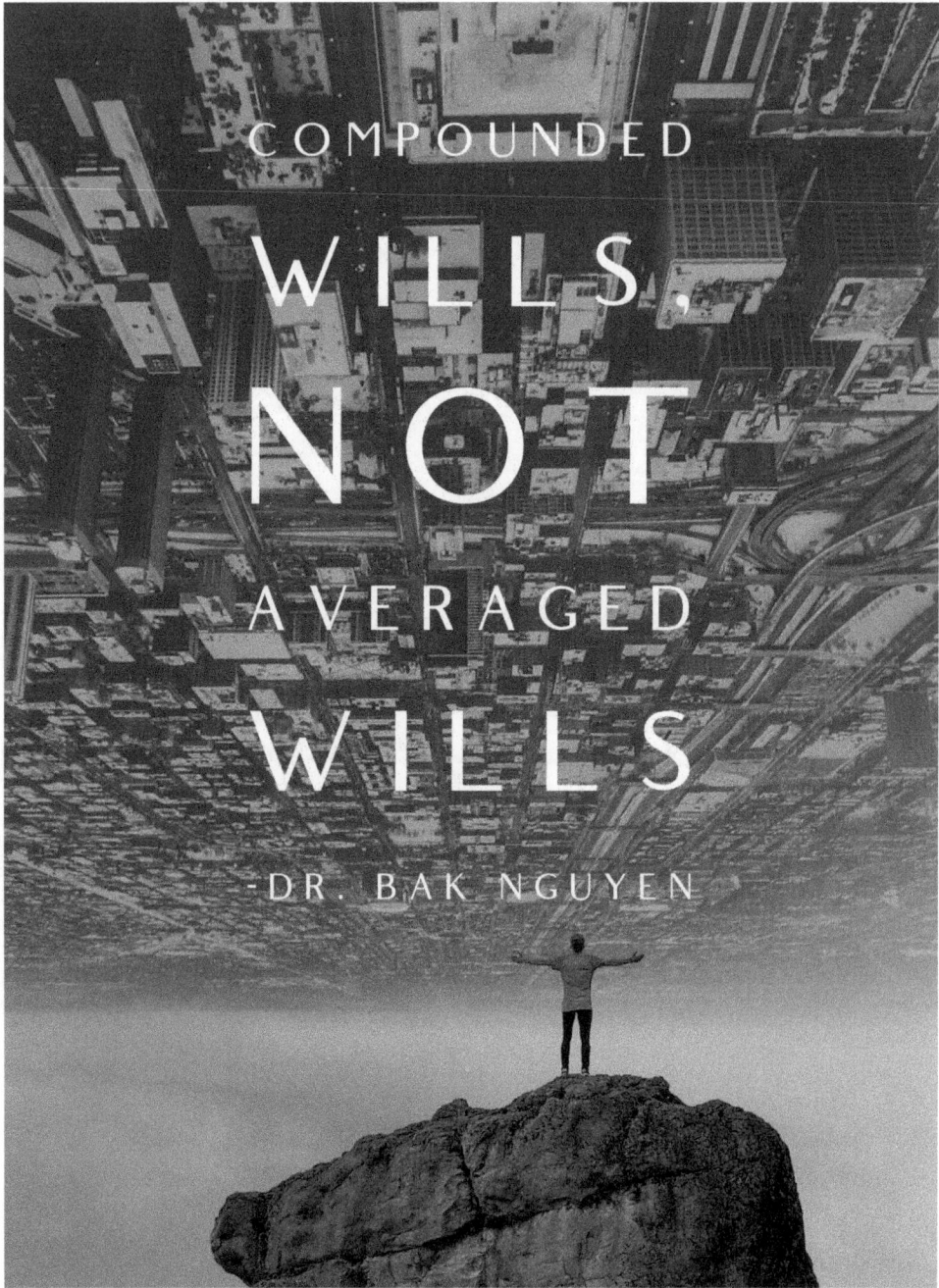

COMPOUNDED
WILLS,
NOT
AVERAGED
WILLS

-DR. BAK NGUYEN

Chapter 5
"History is masterpieced with the palette of Greed. Good and bad, but always great!"
Speech by Dr. Bak Nguyen

It's has been said, « That **Greed**, in a lack of a better word, is good. » It is both wise and right. **Greed** is a powerful emotion, one the strongest with fear, use to motivate and control human behaviors.

Hunters, politicians, stocks brokers all live and die with the laws of **Fear** and the auras of **Greed** etched into their souls. And so do we. We are all in it. Together.

Our world, no matter the country, is all painted in **shades of Greed** and **Fear**. Like black and white, the nuances of **Greed** and **Fear** are used to paint masterpieces, capturing emotional greatness.

Most of our accomplishments through History were immortalized with the palette of **Greed**. Good and evil, but always great! **Greed** and **Fear** are neither good nor bad by themselves, and they only empower what lies within the heart of the contenders.

There is no hiding from those **shades of truth** — **Greed** and **Fear** paint daily, with a disarming precision, our true nature. Still, like what you see in the mirror?

Greed can be useful if shaped into purpose. Desire can serve oneself, and **Greed** can help the many. Not take from the many. **Greed** is hunger evolved to the next stage.

Greed is a fancy label for ambition. **Greed**, at the primary step is called survival. So what is so bad about it? Small minds and naysayers will say otherwise. And still, **Greed** is what keeps them on the path, the **Greed** for attention.

As we move forward from birth to death on the path of life, we balance from right to left to find footing. That's how we scale ourself between **Greed** and **Fear**, one at our right and one at our left.

No angel nor demon, how we choose to paint ourself. Light cannot exist without Darkness nor Heat without Cold, so is **Greed** without **Fear**.

Ascertain as we will all die one day, the difference is how and how fast. How and how quickly we have lived our life. How and how soon we have revealed ourself.

How and how rapidly we have grown... old and wise or sick and senile. So how do you want to walk your path? How will you picture your masterpiece? It has already started. Maybe without you knowing?

Just like life, we started small, from nothing, in the tones of black, of **Fear**. Slowly, we grow and take shape, and we become a stain of color, of hope, of light in that black canvas.

As we become self-aware, we see the potential, and the blackness is infinite, limitless. We can take as much space as we desire.

Greed is abundant. **Greed** is our love for life. **Greed** allows us to move into the direction that we choose, and we can change shades at any time, we are in control.

The trail we left behind is our masterpiece, dedicated to creation. As artists usually are misunderstood, so will we as we are playing with the **shades of Greed**.

The strokes keep defining the canvas, and there is no do-over, there is no eraser. Just a flow of inspiration on the black canvas slowly taking shape into the masterpiece of life, your masterpiece for life.

Fear will urge us to be discreet, to think over each of your strokes, to rethink what we did yesterday, even if there is no do-over nor eraser.

Fear will keep the canvas as black and empty as possible. While **Greed** will push us, let go, to explode to explore both the multitude of shades available and the vastness of the canvas. Bold and noble **Greed** is if, and only if, we stay humble.

In the grand scale of the universe, our masterpiece will find its way into the greatness of Creation. Where we will be the feature and how we will appreciate all depend on what our strokes have left on the canvas, the canvas of life!

Will we be a tiny dot or a big stain? Do we want to be a waste or something people will look up to? We all live life for ourself, every single one of us.

But we can also do more, and we can discover our true ourself while we are making the world better! The more we will elevate the world and our surroundings with our emotions, the more our masterpiece will gain in value in the collection. It is not a race, and it's a matter to take our rightful place in the universe.

Life is a test. Life is a journey. My fellow citizen of the world, make your matter. Make yours great! Empower us with your audacity.

Inspire us with your generosity. Lead us with your love because time is no turning back. And you will be feature anyway. The only difference is where we will be featured.

For the love of life, for the strength of **Hope**, for the future of the legacy of our kind, make something worthwhile.

Citizen of the world, entrepreneurs, **LionHearts**, I salute you!

EVERYTHING ONCE

STARTED

LITTLE.

LITTLENESS,

NOT SMALLNESS

-DR. BAK NGUYEN

Chapter 6
"The curse of Intelligence."
Speech by Dr. Bak Nguyen

To change the world, we have to be smart. This is what we are told. This is sad, not true. The **determination** of a **LionHeart** will suffice to change the world.

But to make it better, really better, our mind can change the path of history if it serves a master, a

LionHeart. This is where the **curse of intelligence** is sealed.

Even if knowledge has the attributes to lead by itself, it surely has the strength to do so, it needs a purpose higher than itself to do good. To look beyond oneself.

As the **LionHeart** dictates what must be, the mind has the power to make it happens, with ease. Together, they make ideas come to life, some times, in the blink of the moment.

When we say that the human spirit is among the most powerful energy of the universe, it is true. True if the spirit is **whole**, if the soul has both the heart and the mind as its counterparts.

As a human being, we are even more ingenious than what nature has given us. We have the ability to combine our spirits to collaborate and have the strongest hearts and the brightest minds moving in the same direction.

Sure, a leader will arise, but that leader is not the sole courageous nor the smartest. He serves as a guardian, to keep pride out of the room, to keep the eyes on the prized purpose.

Failing to understand the dynamics of power between the heart and the mind will have catastrophic consequences.
- Dr. Bak Nguyen

Then, the whole body will suffer the most enormous scars deriving from intelligence, **Pride**. It might succeed for a time, but every time, Pride will be struck down, at a very high cost. **Do not confuse greatness and intelligence**.

Pride is self-awareness of one's intelligence without presence of a purpose for the greater.
- Dr. Bak Nguyen

If you feel pride beating in your heart, be glad. Feel blessed. You are intelligent! You have the power to make things happen. Make sure to embrace the humility to serve first, and embrace yourself fully, because the world needs you.

With humility, intelligence is the sharpest tool that we have at our disposal. With Humility!
- Dr. Bak Nguyen

Humility is not what we think.
Humility is love,
And Humility is the greed for life;

Humility is the hunger to evolve.
Humility is the ambition to be part of the universe
And shine as a whole.

With humility,
Our intelligence will light the way
To abundance!

To make the world a better place,
We need a LionHeart.
To change to world,
We need determination.

To grow the world,
We need imagination and intelligence,
Intelligence married to humility.

That doesn't mean to compromise. The **worst thing** that can happen is to **average intelligence and courage**. The easy way is to please to avoid confrontation. It will take courage to step up, to face adversity, to lead.

A leader will have to stand up and lead the way to greatness, not just through the day. We cannot compromise greatness, and we cannot average talents nor intelligence.

To level up, is the only way to grow!
- Dr. Bak Nguyen

Help those who are behind, but stay true to yourself. No compromise, no average, no pride, with courage, with intelligence and mostly, with **HUMILITY**.

We are great because we have the intelligence to work together. We are strong because we have the knowledge to love and helps each other. We are intelligent because we are growing together. We will thrive because we know that we need each other.

Citizen of the world, entrepreneurs, **LionHearts**, we are all in it together, and that's how we will make it! To the next level, to greatness, to what our children will consider as a natural part of life, of their legacy!

We build with what we have and together, we have everything! To change the world, we need to be smart. Now it's true.

Citizen of the world, entrepreneurs, **LionHearts**, I salute you!

PRIDE

IS SELF-AWARENESS

OF ONE'S

INTELLIGENCE

WITHOUT PRESENCE OF

A PURPOSE FOR

THE GREATER

-DR. BAK NGUYEN

Chapter 7
"The Gift of Resilience"
Speech by Dr. Bak Nguyen

Life is a journey, a Journey of Empowerment
- Dr. Bak Nguyen

Life is a journey. Leadership is destiny . As life can be abundant, full of friends and love, leadership is a lonely path. Because the leader always has to move forward, even if he is the only one to feel the need.

A true leader, a **LionHeart** serves more than he dictates. He inspires respect, not idolization.

The great leaders are the ones who don't want to lead.
- Socrate

Because they are to busy achieving their destiny to stop and give orders. If their achievements are what the world needs, we've just found the perfect mind to lead us until completion.

As soon as it is done, he will leave. Because, he needs to follow his heart to his next adventure, to achieve his subsequent greatness.

He has guided us, inspired us, he will be remembered. We shouldn't regret him nor try to delay his departure. We should be grateful and wish him luck on his next adventure.

Because, we have retained the best part of him, of that leader, of that hero, of that entrepreneur, his **empowerment** and **creativity**.

The journey of a true leader is to empower those around him to achieve their full potential, to show them the vastness of the Horizon beyond the valley.

It is not merely out of nobility of character that a **LionHeart** will help to rise those who are ready.

His nature dictates him to stay ahead and to continue to push the limits further. That's his only way to fulfillment, to happiness.

Victory is in the race.
- Dr. Bak Nguyen

He is not competing against any of us but himself, to see how strong his will is, and how far his heart will lead him.

On the way, a **LionHeart** knows too well that nothing will last if he stands alone. That's why he will naturally empower those who are ready to listen, to have access to that divine force inside of them.

There are not followers; they are his teammates in a race, for the present moment.

As in any team, the strength of the team lies in the weakest links. That why he empowers, that's why he will inspire. No unit can last forever as each of the **LionHearts** has to pursue their destiny.

That's why **leadership is momentarily**, even with the power of **momentum**, the race will eventually end, and the team disbanded.

So if we have the chance to meet a **LionHeart**, that's our cue to be ready. Ready to learn, to work, to improve ourself, just by standing next to him.

By trying to walk in his footsteps, for the time he is still within reach. As he inspired the best out of us, we will be climbing to heights we never thought possible. Sure, as we become stronger, the envy to beat him at his own game will strike our heart.

Embrace that playfulness because the day that we will beat him, we should embrace his brotherhood and thank him for his patience and generosity. We won't have much time, and he will be gone soon — every single time.

The time we have together is priceless. The achievements, if we've genuinely connected, will last for ages. Above all, his true greatness is that he has just spawned a new **LionHeart**.

To our destiny, we must go and now, we know.

Until next time. That's true leadership. We must recognize it and empower it. Leadership is not a prestige, it's a burden.

The glory is not to sit on the top, but to move the average up.
- Dr. Bak Nguyen

The shame is not to leave but to have missed that the race has ended, long ago. The **LionHeart** does not divide, it identifies. The **LionHeart** does not compare; it connects.

Citizen of the world, entrepreneurs, **LionHearts**, the fate of our collective future depends on the greatness of our leaders, on the size of every single soul on the team.

Everyone counts; we are all in this together. Should we recognize who we are clearly, we should act accordingly and begin to grow. If we can lift the **band of pride** and jealousy, we can touch the sky and live out our **destiny** until it becomes a **legacy**!

This is a single journey, an individual one that each of us will need to decide for himself. How much longer will you doubt yourself and fight over the carrot instead of rising up and go for the elephants?

How much longer will you buried your feet and head in the ground thinking about growing? Even if we each have our unique destiny, we are all seeking the same air, a chance for happiness.

Whatever your joy is, you have to stand up and reach for it yourself. No one will do it for you. But you don't have to do it all by yourself, alone the whole way.

Now you know. Now you see. Now you are ready to rise.

The greatness of our world is the compounded greatness of every single one of us.
- Dr. Bak Nguyen

Let aim for the stars and shine as a whole, together! Citizen of the world, entrepreneurs, **LionHearts**, I salute you!

WE CAN'T CHANGE WHAT WAS. WE CAN ONLY HAVE THE WISDOM TO EASE THE WAY

-DR. BAK NGUYEN

Chapter 8
"A Taste of Freedom"
Speech by Dr. Bak Nguyen

Freedom, will, loyalty, they are all related to one's quest of identity. We will have many quests in our lifetime, but there are three universal quests:

- The Quest of Identity

- The Quest of Happiness

- The Quest for Freedom

Most of us will spend their lifetime looking to walk and triumph from those three quests. So what are those?

The **Quest of Identity** is our first conscious quest. It begins with **Pride**, that lie that we call **self-love**. That day that we choose to bite into the Apple, for the promise of freedom, to find out who we are and what we are made of.

We felt it was a natural step of growth, and each of us will have to walk the path to understand the significance of our name and the values in our hearts.

The **Quest of identity** is the Quest to find one's heart. Sooner or later, we have to walk the path, often leaving behind most of what we knew to grow, to understand.

This quest, we must do alone. Even if we might have allies on the way, we are the only one that could push the door and get through. As we have found ourselves and accepted our purpose, we are then ready to start our legend.

One's story can only begin as one's quest for identity ends.
- Dr. Bak Nguyen

And our legend will start with the next quest, the **Quest of Happiness**. The **Quest of Happiness** is often confused with the **pursuit of identity**.

Happiness is not free. Is it? From childhood, we were born fundamentally happy. If we had a love of our mom and dad, we knew **Love**, and if we were hungry, we felt our mom's warm milk on our lips, if we were cold, we had the certainty of her presence to protect us.

Not everyone had that chance. To those, they have been stripped of their most valued legacy from life, first love. To them, we must fix the injustice, we must love and comfort.

For the rest of us, happiness was a natural given state. So what happened? Why do we spend a big part of our life in the search for joy if we had it in the first place?

I wish the answer were an easy one. Because we **confused happiness and identity** because we didn't differentiate **freedom from pride**, because we thought that love was free.

Love is free, but it requires us to give and receive. It's a two ways relationship. From our parents, we took what we could, not until much later in life that we understand what they gave us.

Gratitude tells much about one's character. If there is no Gratitude, there is no hope and therefore, no future.
- Dr. Bak Nguyen

We thought that we would be happy finding ourselves. Unfortunately, it was false beliefs, induced by Pride. We will only have a shoot to Happiness once we've found ourselves.

The day we have kissed Pride, we made a hole in our soul, and we spend years trying to fill that hole. A hole we call **destiny**.

Is the whole quest of identity a mistake to begin with? The error was to have a bite in the **Apple of Pride**. Now, we have to make the most out of it, as soon as possible, we need to fill the hole in our soul before we get used to it and start giving a meaning to its presence.

Our mind will do that, and it will rationalize the void to provide it with meaning and purpose, even value. That's not greatness, that's a **rationalization**. It might help, but it is a lie.

So the **quest of happiness** is, in reality, the **redemption** for our pride, the journey to get back in paradise. That quest won't be easy, but it doesn't have to be harder than it already is.

If we embrace the kingdom of Gratitude, we have the map that will lead us back to paradise.
- Dr. Bak Nguyen

The future is a part of the past of our past. Move ahead with confidence, because you know where it leads, we were there once. But now, we must earn our way back. That's our legend, the person we will have become to make our way again.

And the **quest for Freedom**? That's the primal lie we've been served. But now that we are on our own, we have the choice to pity ourselves and cry upon our lost or get back up there.

That's freedom, the burden to know that it is upon us to make the difference, for ourselves, by ourselves. Is **freewill** a curse or a gift? Really.

Since it's too late for regrets, we must embrace it as a gift, the one chance that we have to find the path back to paradise.

The journey will strip us from our innocence, and the miles will strengthen our spirit, so we know that happiness is really what we want.

The challenges will sharpen our minds to understand the fabric of the universe. We are neither good nor bad, simply trying to find our way home. Our choices will label us as good or bad.

Along the way, we will find love, and we will be loved, we will give love. That's our way back, to give what we have received. To live through the eyes of our child, the beauty of innocence, of true happiness is our redemption. We will embrace that gift.

But Pride lies deep in our blood. It resides in our child, waiting to awake, once again. And we will be powerless to see our child bites in the **Apple of Pride**.

> **We cannot change what was.**
> **We can only have the wisdom**
> **to ease the way.**
> **- Dr. Bak Nguyen**

Citizen of the world, entrepreneurs, **LionHearts**, since we cannot change the past, I urge you to embrace our destiny and to make it great!

Include everyone ready and make of your journey the chance of a lifetime! If we are condemned to walk one quest after the next, feel blessed because we are not dead yet!

Let's make the journey so exciting that Pride will feel like it has done us a favor! There is no better revenge than to strike doubt in the heart of Pride itself!

Yes, we have free will, we know what we are thanks to the **wisdom of Gratitude**, we know the way to happiness. It is to accept our destiny and celebrate it with joy and love. We will make the most of what we've received, and we are grateful for it.

Citizen of the world, entrepreneurs, **LionHearts**, light the way to happiness with freedom, with love, with respect. That's who we are.

Citizen of the world, entrepreneurs, **LionHearts**, I salute you!

ONE'S LEGEND CAN
ONLY BEGIN
THE DAY
ONE'S QUEST OF
IDENTITY
IS OVER.

-DR. BAK NGUYEN

Chapter 9
"The words of Success."
Speech by Dr. Bak Nguyen

My fellow citizen, we can be great, together or alone, it's our choice to make. In our heart, we decide who we are and so, what will be.

To do so, we need the support of our mind. We need to believe in our success, and we need to see the bright future. We need to embrace the present and leave the past behind.

Every day, the words and thoughts we use and hear will strengthen our beliefs. They will construct the blueprint of our hearts. In turn, our beliefs will shape our desires and views. Those desires and views will paint our horizon.

The horizon, your horizon is the canvas for your ambition. The ambition to grow, the ambition to be, the ambition to live life to the fullest.

To be hungry is to love what Life has to offer. To be curious is to know the vastness of the horizon. To be generous is to know with certainty that Life is abundant.

So choose carefully the words you are feeding yourself with, they will make you or break you, while you eat, while you sleep, while you wait.

Take **Generosity** for example, and if one is generous and kind in his heart, he will give without holding back, he will not even think otherwise. He will feel great giving, he will feel **strong** and **tall**.

That day, he has touched a **primal fiber** of the Universe. That day, he will never go in need again, because he has risen above the carrot.

His mind has outgrown its previous canvas. He still has to hunt for the elephants, but he has touched a new dimension, his mind has discovered a new reality.

And never, he can go back to what he was and what he once ate. Know that what we eat make us who we are.

**To feel is to grow
To say is to know
Now, you know**
- Bak Nguyen

The **WORDS OF SUCCESS** are powerful, so are the words of regrets and the words of fear. They don't go together, and they don't fit in the same puzzle. And that's our blessing, that's our warning.

We have to choose our theme because they don't overlap. We cannot borrow a little from each one because they will then add up to nothing.

We have to choose, and we have to move forward, leaving the rest behind. Once we've chosen our theme, we will give in and become the theme ourself.

The **WORDS OF SUCCESS**, of positivity, open up a world of possibilities that can be our new reality. That's the **POWER OF THE MIND**. Even **Time** can be bended if we have the **STRENGTH OF WISDOM**.

Success is a choice, Success is a journey, Success is stylish, Success is a great feeling, Success starts with a single word.

Citizen of the world, entrepreneurs, **LionHearts**, whatever we choose, we make our destiny. We can master our destiny or bear its weight on our shoulders, it is for us to choose.

We can mount the **HORSE OF FREEDOM** or fear the **BEAST OF DOUBTS**, we choose. We can walk this world with our head looking at the sky or at our feet, we choose.

We have embraced freedom, and we are in control. So be careful, be thoughtful, choose wisely, because there is no turning back.

There is so much in the world to see, to taste, to share. There is even more in our hearts to touch, to give, to grow. We have the power to choose, and we have the power to succeed.

So choose. Choose now, choose to go. You have everything to lose not to choose. Choose to raise hope, choose to rise above yourself, choose to make the world kind and great, choose to leave behind what once was.

It takes courage, and it takes vision, it takes the first step, to embrace.

Citizen of the world, entrepreneurs, **LionHearts**, choose, walk the **PATH OF FREEDOM** and lead the way to Greatness, to Abundance.

Citizen of the world, entrepreneurs, **LionHearts**, I salute you!

WITH HUMILITY, INTELLIGENCE IS THE SHARPEST TOOL THAT WE HAVE AT OUR DISPOSAL. WITH HUMILITY!

-DR. BAK NGUYEN

Chapter 10
"The Smell of Death"
Speech by Dr. Bak Nguyen

The **SMELL OF DEATH,** how could we find empowerment from the **SMELL OF DEATH**, how can we put a positive twist to it?

The challenge summarizes the spirit of a real **LionHeart** and entrepreneur. Never back down from a challenge, make the most of what is given, good or bad, it's up to us to make it great. So is the **SMELL OF DEATH**.

Death is a shadow, a fear, and eventually a promise. Why should we be scared of a shadow if we stand in the light, why embrace fear if fear only has a grip if we allow it to? Why be fearful of a promise when we know with certainty the outcome?

But wait, we can still make a difference and live, fully, until death comes knocking. We will be so busy that we won't even notice that we've been released from duty, from fun.

Death can afraid of some of us. And that's all right, as long as you run faster than death, you will have outraced it and live to fight another day, to achieve your destiny!

Cheating is bad, but cheating death can be uplifting!
- Dr. Bak Nguyen

We don't take no for an answer; why take it here? Dare to challenge the fear of death, look it into his eyes and say, no, not yet, not until time runs out on us!

With our **LionHeart**, we have a way to bend time, and we can still run and beat death another day, again. Arrogance is terrible, but take pride upon outrunning Death, and it will keep us sharp and motivated.

So do it. Run and do. Run and don't stop. Embrace Life to the fullest. Don't hold anything back, for the day that we will look death in the eye, we won't have anything left to regret!

Be grateful, make the shadow of death a daily reminder to our life, our opportunities, our abundance. Death will keep us on our toes, will keep boredom and complacency away.

The worst punishment known to mankind is to have a date with Death and keep waiting until it shows up! To those souls, I feel your pain, your solitude. Please remember that you can always choose to get up and start running again. Where there is hope, there is life.

Death can be difficult and do the unexpected, but why care if we are powerless? So care for what you have the power to change, care for what your Will can influence. We do not have enough room to care for death.

Because Death will only care for us the day, it comes. Before, Death won't even bother to know our name. So to fear Death or to wait for it is to love and respect someone who will not love us back! So again, why care?

Even once the **SMELL OF DEATH** catches us, we are not out until we are out! Give it your last shoot, your best shot! From what we know, maybe if we impress Death enough, it might lose its focus for a while and let us escape, once more!

That tale is a sure winner for the fire camp and the bedtime stories. Children will sing songs about our tales for the ages to come.

Don't embrace Death, but be grateful, because Death made us great! The fear of Death pushed us forward. The **SMELL OF DEATH** reminded us to run faster and faster.

The fear of Death is worse than Death itself
- Dr. Bak Nguyen

Citizen of the world, entrepreneurs, **LionHearts**, we are blessed, blessed with life, blessed with opportunities, blessed with time.

We are blessed because we can feel our hearts beating in our chests, because we can still give our love to make someone smile. No one is useless for as long as it can still make another smile. Remember that.

Death is a sure thing. But when, that's not written yet, not until it's too late. So why care?
- Dr. Bak Nguyen

Citizen of the world, entrepreneurs, **LionHearts**, go, cheat Death, live your life fearless because Death has no power over us until we give up.

We have the ability, we have the will, and we will make the difference. Citizen of the world, entrepreneurs, **LionHearts**, I salute you!

THE GLORY
IS NOT
TO SIT
ON TOP,
BUT
TO MOVE
THE
AVERAGE
UP

-DR. BAK NGUYEN

Chapter 11
"The Breath of Generosity"
Speech by Dr. Bak Nguyen

One's character and merits are in the size of his heart. Some are bigger than others. Some start small and stay small, while others will grow into **LionHearts**.

We all have little hearts as we came into this world. The chance to grow our heart is always available to each one of us as we choose to grow by opening our hearts and minds. We choose to embrace abundance as we allow our heart to **skip a beat**, from time to time.

Love will do just that. Love will grow your heart and skip a beat once in a while. That's how we feel alive; that's how we taste the greatness of life, with love.

To be generous is to love, ourself, and others.
- Dr. Bak Nguyen

We love because it makes us grow, because it helps us feel more of the world, because it opens our eyes to new possibilities.

Generosity is not selfless, but it's still noble. Sure, sometime, we will get hurt, and love will not have give as expected. But love, thanks to its generosity, is abundant. Our heart will heal just fine.

Even with scars, a healed heart is more attractive than a brand new one.
- Dr. Bak Nguyen

Our heart is not meant to be kept safe and new. It is intended to explore and accumulate feelings and experiences. The more we give, the more we will have. Those maths never lie.

A LionHeart does not divide; it multiplies.
- Dr. Bak Nguyen

The more it beats, the more it is. The more it grows, the stronger it gets. Most **LionHearts** don't even know the math, and they don't care, there are and make it be!

Just like breathing air, the breath of Generosity is second nature as we grow into a **LionHeart**.

The **Generosity** of a heart is the **scale** in which **Life is measured**. A strong heart will matter. A big heart will lift the world with its breath alone. A **LionHeart** is a hope upon which our world of tomorrow depends on.

From the lion, hearts will beat the rhythm of love, will shine the courage to save the day, will shy Death away for another day!

Greatness is not something we see, it is something we feel. The importance is in the heart. And a **LionHeart** won't feel it. It will, but it won't know that it is called greatness. Because a **LionHeart** is always looking towards the future, what's passed has no bearing over him.

A **LionHeart** breathes generosity, that's its nature, that's its selfishness, that's its pride. Even if those words have no meaning to him. It's only the way others look at him and describe him.

Citizen of the world, entrepreneurs, **LionHearts**, do you know the size of your heart? Does it weight in the balance as you thought it would or as you wish it would?

You decide, you choose the size of your heart. You can decide to keep it closed, and as is or open it up and allow it to grow. It is not free but uplifting, and it will take efforts, not sacrifice, it will require courage so it can scare death away in a whisper.

The **WHISPER OF A LIONHEART** is more powerful than the will of a fearful crowd. Be fearless, not nervous. Be courageous, not shy. Be contagious, not corrupted.

Because to be generous is to master wealth and power. To be generous illustrates how confident one is. To be liberal is to trust in Life and ourself.

Love is a feeling, and Generosity is a state of mind. Like success, it can be taught and mastered. The **BREATH OF GENEROSITY** is both powerful and noble.

It opens more doors than it closes. It cultivated one's soul to be ready to take on bigger responsibilities. It forces the smallness of one

heart to turn into greatness. The power of
Generosity is to give in order to be, and to
receive more from God.

The **BREATH OF GENEROSITY** is what we've received
from mother nature. That's how seeds grow into
trees, that's how seas keep feeding us. That's
how the sun shines upon us every day.

So to be a **LionHeart** is to be part of nature, to
become a force of nature. It's more than great,
it's natural!

Citizen of the world, entrepreneurs, **LionHearts**, I
feel privileged to walk among you, to be part of
the greater, of the whole. My heart beats with
yours so we, together, will make this world better!

Citizen of the world, entrepreneurs, **LionHearts**, I
salute you!

LIFE CAN

BE ABOUT US IF WE MAKE

IT ABOUT OTHERS FIRST.

-DR. BAK NGUYEN

Chapter 12
"The Legacy of the LionHeart"
Speech by Dr. Bak Nguyen

The race to matter, we've all felt it at some point in our lives. The desire to be heard, to make the difference, to do something worth telling.

Sometimes, it is to help the many, and often, it is to fix the obvious, the injustice. That envy burning inside, it's your **LionHeart** calling.

Complacency, the **fear of rejection**, and **self-doubt** will try to silence the calling to rally. It is the whisper of a **LionHeart**. We will feel it, we will hear it. We can choose to ignore it, but we will feel it.

We can choose to awake or to stay still. Either way, we will never be the same. After the calling, we either join the race and grow with strength or stay behind, nostalgic of what could have been, of what we could become.

It is then, that self-doubt and fear will have taken over our hearts. We were free to choose. Now we are prisoners of our own heart. Be warned, now you know.

Nothing in this life will leave us unchanged. Either we advanced, or we've been passed over, left behind to see others rise. It was our choice. It is our choice. That's the power we have, the energy we were born with, the **FREEDOM TO CHOOSE**. Citizen of the world, choose wisely.

Our true calling is one of love, of devotion. To be able to give ourself and join in the movement, the whole. That's how Life flows in our veins; that's how our heart celebrates its vitality.

To matter means nothing unless it is to matter to others!
- Dr. Bak Nguyen

To matter to one or to the many is still to matter. Greatness is the same; the idea of growth will occur in both cases. It's intoxicating, charming, as we started to touch another life, another soul, for the better.

Our own soul starts to glow. We will feel it, feel the depth of the love of Life. People will see it, see the intensity of the light of self-awareness.

That day, we've started to matter. That day, we've grown into a pole of gravity that people will be drawn to, will look up to. A force of nature that is, a primal element that people will find a use for.

As we lead the many, remember, **LionHearts**, that our purpose is to serve them until they have grown and can go on their own. They might never be fully ready, but they will have grown, just standing next to us, **LionHearts**. And it will still only be the beginning of our rise.

The **LionHeart** knows no limit, its growth can be limitless, as the vastness of the canvas allows it. We will move on to our next adventure, to matter again, differently, to another crowd, in another world.

And how do we know that we have a **LionHeart**? We don't. No one with a **LionHeart** knows. We will slowly realize our true nature from the contact with others. From their eyes, one will see our true reflection, the glares of the **LionHeart**.

The journey is opened to everyone and anyone. So if you hear the calling, give in. Start to grow and enjoy the charms of kinetic. After all, you are a citizen of the world, and this is your world! This is our world.

It's our choice to make, our chance to take. Stand up, wake the path, do and eventually, stop and see in their eyes what you've we've become.

Yes, we have to become a **LionHeart**. We have to grow into one. No one is just born with a **LionHeart**. The **LionHeart** lives and dies with the wind of movement, of kinetic. It is stronger as it beats to matter. It ages and become heavier as it slows down its pace and leaves the race.

The death of a **LionHeart** is to be condemned to stay still, to stop. That's why, all its life, the **LionHeart** will search for greatness and achievements. Because it's how it stays strong, how it stays alive. A curse or a blessing? It all depends on the eyes judging. It's a matter of choice and values.

And why matter? Because we are not alone. Greatness can be achieved from everywhere, from one's quest of solitude to the salvation of nations.

Greatness is not in the size of the numbers, but the audacity of the reach.
- Dr. Bak Nguyen

There is a pearl of old wisdom saying: "Alone, we go fast; together, we go far." The **LionHeart** knows that everything he touches will change, but for it to last, he needs the many to join in his movement.

Even if he can build most of the dream himself, he needs to share his vision for it to grow. Once out, the vision has a life of its own. Some times, it will even outgrow the **LionHeart** who gave it life! Just as a child who will eventually outgrow his parents. Proud and joy will be. A true **LionHeart** will let go, will let be.

For its vision to happen and to matter, the **LionHeart** needs a team to keep the legacy alive. That's why he will slow down, help, nurture, and teach. It will also be a good opportunity to inspire the little ones and spawn some young **LionHearts** on the way.

Citizen of the world, entrepreneurs, you all have the choice to find out about your heart, your destiny. Embrace it with passion, and you might find a **LionHeart** beating in your chest.

The whole way, we were the servant, the vessel, the tool for the greater good. The result is not about us, and it's about them. The journey happens with them, but the journey, the journey is about us.

About how we choose to matter, how we handle the race and ultimately how we become a

LionHeart. Just like the **SMELL OF DEATH** will keep us sharp on our toes, the need to matter will stir the way of our ambition and make us embrace our destiny. Fully.

To be kind, to be generous, to flexible, to be smart, to be strong, those are the legacies of the **LionHeart**.

Citizen of the world, entrepreneurs, **LionHearts**, I salute you!

TO DIVIDE
IS NOT
DIVINE.
TO
SUBTRACT
IS NOT
NATURAL

-DR. BAK NGUYEN

Chapter 13
"The scars of Innocence."
Speech by Dr. Bak Nguyen

The scars of Innocence or of naivety are both the stripes of courage and a remainder our the past failures. Sometimes deep and painful, those scars serve as storytellers of our journey.

Were they all necessary? No. But they made us into who we are. We should accept them and not try to hide them away. They help keep track of our journey to greatness.

The Scars hold more than the memories of knowledge, and they keep the colors and the smell of emotions too.
- Dr. Bak Nguyen

There is neither pride, not shame to bear the scars of Innocence. They are just part of our legend. To take advantage of them, we have to move forward with a light heart and experiences, not with eternal pain and trauma.

Like a heart needs to beat to grow, our soul needs innocence to try new things, to learn to fly. If our mind takes over too soon, we will learn to fear and embrace the self-imposed limits to avoid repeating pain.

Our minds may have favored the survival instinct, but our heart, curious, will always be longing for more, wondering what is beyond. Both have good intentions, and the matter is in the measure.

Innocence is the ignorance of those safeguards for survival.
- Dr. Bak Nguyen

To jump head first, to taste more of Life, to thrive, that's innocence. Some would call it **courage** if they were focusing on the limits while we were looking at the horizon.

The other would call it **ignorance** if they were looking at their scars. To us, **LionHearts**, it was simply a step forward. A step we wanted to take, a step we may love or regret.

Again, there is not much of a difference if we keep moving forward. The only difference is in the speed we will deploy to go through, and the time we will spend asking for more. It's part of the past anyway.

The mind will etch the scars into our heart to remember, to avoid tasting the same bitterness again. Can we call that smart?
- Dr. Bak Nguyen

To suffer a little more now in order to avoid suffering later? That sounds smart, but who can enjoy it? Really. We were wrong, we got through,

and they want to punish us a little more for it?!
For our own good? Not me.

**I have enough from my journey to add on
extra weight and pain. I don't have room
to reinforce fear in my heart.**
- Dr. Bak Nguyen

We, need to heal and to stay light to jump in
again and eventually, to fly. We want to go faster,
higher, pushing the limits. We should minimize
the pain, not amplify it!

We should forget the past, not etch it in our soul
forever! The day we will fly, the scars, all of them,
won't matter, and they surely won't help. So why
suffer more than necessary?

Innocence will drive us to do crazy things, beautiful things, dangerous things. As they say, what does not kill you will make you stronger.

So yes, your **innocence** will put you out there and strengthen your heart. It will forge your **resilience** and will keep you opened to the **vastness of Life**.

To say **YES** as default and taste most of what Life offers. You'll eat more of Life, see more of Life, know more from Life. Some things you'll love more than others, some, you'll hate. But now you know. You've grown all the way!

Citizen of the world, entrepreneurs, **LionHearts**, don't fear Life, embrace it. If we accept Life as a whole, that Life cannot exist without death, that sweet taste better when we tasted sour before, that joy can shine through any sadness, we will accumulate scars and experiences.

The **SCARS OF INNOCENCE** and the **WISDOM OF EXPERIENCE**, are the recognition for our odyssey. As we are aware of the value of Time, we won't do the same mistake twice, and we won't bite the same bitterness again, thanks to our mind.

We need to keep it in check, not just to surrender most of our freedom and judgment, thinking that it will safeguard them. Actually, it will safeguard them, it will keep them from trying and tasting anything new, sometimes forever.

To embrace Life is to accept the eventuality of death. That's what makes it so exciting, so alive!

To love is to respect one's right to find out more of oneself. To care is to be there when one's require an opened heart to share with.
- Dr. Bak Nguyen

We will be called to build the world of tomorrow with our hands and perception of reality. We will shape it with our heart and what we valued most.

The more we know, the more we have to build with. The next generations will enjoy it as what always was, as a natural state of Life, given.

We wanted to provide them with the best of what Life has to offer: **joy**, **health**, and **comfort**. We wish them the best of Life: **freedom** and **growth**.

If we are strong and generous enough to trust that we've raised them well and have prepared them for Life, we will wish them luck and let them be! As other once did for us.

We will show them our scars of experiences and entertain them with the stories of our adventures. We will share with them knowledge and wisdom.

All they will hear is how great was our journey, of how badly they want to taste it for themselves. And until we run out of time, we too will be seduced again by the **MAGIC OF LIFE**, and we will embrace our next adventure with an opened heart, with innocence.

Citizen of the world, entrepreneurs, **LionHearts**, I salute you!

THE UNIVERSE

IS ALWAYS EXPANDING,

SO SHOULD OUR MINDS AND HEARTS

-DR. BAK NGUYEN

Chapter 14
"The Reach of Positivity"
Speech by Dr. Bak Nguyen

Ambition is the thirst of the win. That thirst never goes away. Each win will feed the thirst to grow bigger. So the attitude by default of a **LionHeart** is to look for the win.

Went he hunts, he won't back down until he got his meal. To do so, to win consistently, we must believe in ourself, our potential. Until we've done it, it's new, and it's uncertain, we can't be sure.

Innocence will allow us to go to the edge and jump without fear, without hesitation, not overthinking the unknown.
- Dr. Bak Nguyen

A heart free of fear can grow wings in a few heartbeats if its believes strongly. We jumped headfirst with the certainty that we will make it. We don't see the dangers, the pain, nor the failures.

We see just the next obstacle to overcome. If we fall, we will get back on our feet as fast as we fell, with more determination to get through the wall.

Our intelligence will serve our Will to succeed. And that's what will be because we saw it, because we believe in ourself, because we won't stop. That's the **POWER OF POSITIVITY**.

POSITIVITY is our plan on the battlefield, the blueprint in our mind to overcome whatever we face. The **POWER OF POSITIVITY** will keep our focus on the win.

The **WORDS OF POSITIVITY** will forge our spirit and train our mind daily to know that we are, and because we are, it will be. Nothing is out of reach; nothing is impossible. That's the **REACH OF POSITIVITY**.

That's how a **LionHeart** comes to be, believing in **positivity**.

Sometimes **doubt** will arise. If our heart knows itself and knows where lies its loyalty, doubt will not last long. Our **LionHeart** will dictate the course of actions, the course that will matter to others.

Sometimes we will fail, and the fall will hurt. Sometimes they will face resistance from those we are trying to help. Every time, we will get through.

Sometimes we will have to take down the **WALL OF FEAR**, other times, we will strike down the **CURTAINS OF JEALOUSY**. We know our mission, and our dedication to win will lead the charge.

Don't stand in the way of a loyal heart because there is no victory possible.
- Dr. Bak Nguyen

If it is not strong enough, the **LionHeart** will get stronger with the scars accumulating on its back. If it is not big enough, give it time, it will grow even bigger. Because the **LionHeart** does more than talk, it acts and moves on.

If it is not smart enough, its innocence will push it to dive headfirst and it will learn, fast. **Courageous** and candid, it will get to the bottom of the matter faster than anyone expected it. It was courageous because it simply never heard the whisper of fear.

Speed is the intangible quality of a **LionHeart**, a smart and loyal **LionHeart**. It moves fast to keep doubt and fear from it heart. It moves fast to build its **impact**, its **momentum**.

As it gains in speed, its strength multiple faster than it can count, but it is well aware of the power building up in its heart. It is all possible because its heart has no room for pride. If wasn't about him, it was about mattering, to others.

Citizen of the world, entrepreneurs, **LionHearts**, this is how societies are built. This is how greatness takes root. This is how dreams cease to exist because they have materialized into natural states.

This is how **Hope** will always shine through, because of greatness, because of goodness, because of the inspiration of **the legends of the LionHearts**.

The difference lies only in the size of each heart.
- Dr. Bak Nguyen

Age won't matter for as long as the heart still lives in the **AGE OF INNOCENCE**. Anything is possible. That's the **REACH OF POSITIVITY**. That's the power of the **LionHeart**.

Citizen of the world, entrepreneurs, **LionHearts**, I salute you.

ONE IS NO WHOLE. ONE IS NOT UNITY

-DR. BAK NGUYEN

Chapter 15
"The Hunt of Salvation"
Speech by Dr. Bak Nguyen

From our childhood, we've been told to follow the rules. Some, before us had not, and they all suffered terribly. We need to redeem ourselves.

We have sinned. Only with hard work and devotion, we might find forgiveness. Salvation is accessible to all, and one only needs to want it!

Salvation is universal. Is it hope or a great lie? The recipe is known to all, to erase our sins before we die.
- Dr. Bak Nguyen

We will die, but have we really sinned? That's the lie. They started telling us what is good, and what is evil. They made it sounds worst, calling it sins.

A mistake, a mistake can happen. A mistake will happen if you are alive and looking to evolve. That's natural, that how we grow. Mistakes have to happen for one to learn to walk, run, and fly.

Mistake is the soul of education, mistakes are the chapters of training, upon mistakes are built the stairway to heaven. But a sin, a sin is a stain on the soul. A sin is a hole in the fabric of the universe.

Have we really sin?
Who is telling?
Worst, why are we listening?
- Dr. Bak Nguyen

To keep us in check, to stay in control, they taught us just that, that we were born with sin on our soul, and we have to start to walk our redemption.

From the goodness of their hearts, they will show us the way. It's an offer, but it wasn't a choice. If needed, they will force it down our throats. It might work for a while, but no one's freedom can be raped for that long without eventually rising up violently and take back control.

And again, they were one step ahead of us, they manipulated a safeguard of our mind and turned it against us. They corrupted **FEAR** and make it into our worst enemy.

FEAR was supposed to keep us from making the same mistake again. **FEAR** was designed by the Universe to be a kind hand, to help us grow, to allow us to gain in speed.

They've succeeded to turn **FEAR** upside down. Today, **FEAR** slows us down. Our chains are called roots, and our prison is celebrated as security, our cellmates are named neighbors.

Have a look at the forest, have a look at the trees, and you will see the lies. At some point in the past, flying was a natural state of evolution. Today, it's a secret privilege labeled fantasy.

But we, citizen of the world, entrepreneurs and **LionHearts**, are ingenious. We've adapted, and we've evolved. We found ways to make the most out of those chains and gave meaning to our roots.

We even find new strengths to them. We made improvements to landscape the forest and make it welcoming and warm. We've gone a long way since the beginning of Time, since the origin of sins, since the realms of civilization.

We went such a long way that today, some of us have adapted so well that our nature has morphed at a cellular level into that tree, strong thanks to our roots.

Others, even if they have lost their wings, are still looking at the sky and daydream until they jump and go for their destiny. We call them entrepreneurs, eagles.

Together, we made the most out of our legacy and, when it was possible, avoid the bloody revolutions that our raped freedom is screaming for.

Our world is not black and white nor good or bad. We made sure of that, by adapting.
- Dr. Bak Nguyen

We can not change the past nor deny the legacy we inherited. We can only evolve with what we were given, and what is available.

Citizen of the world, it is too late and frugal to revolt now, since we'll be revolting against a big part of ourselves and our accomplishments as a whole.

It is not complacency, and it is the **RECOGNITION OF EVOLUTION**. But we can do better and build upon the hopes of the past generations.

We can make the most out of the forest, harvesting strengths from the roots while breathing from the **perspective of the eagles**.

The eagles eventually will need to rest and feed on the roots as the forest will need to evolve and grow from the catch of the eagles and the lions.

Lions, eagles and trees, we are all in this together, as a whole. We are born fundamentally neutral, neither good or bad. Let's get rid of the corruption and stop labeling each other.

The secret of the evolution of mankind lies in the wisdom of working together.
- Dr. Bak Nguyen

Citizen of the world, entrepreneurs, **LionHearts**, we all stay hungry from the **quest for salvation**, together, eagles, trees, lions we can hunt, hunt to evolve, hunt to feast, hunt to know each other and hunt to discover our true nature.

It doesn't matter if you are a tree, an eagle, or a lion, we need all attributes to be stronger, as a whole. Each of us, as will have to play of role.

Leadership, once, was about leading the many to conquer with strength. Today, leadership is about **honoring our freedom** and taking actions to evolve and **thrive as a whole**.

We have evolved wiser since the **ages of war**. We won't make it otherwise.

Citizen of the world, entrepreneurs, **LionHearts**, get rid of the corruption, of the labeling and give in. Put in your essence and passion and we will thrive.

Life is abundant, and we can taste all of it together.
- Dr. Bak Nguyen

After all, what is a party if not the gathering of all to celebrate Life?

Citizen of the world, entrepreneurs, **LionHearts**, I salute you.

FREE
AND
WILL.
WE
HAVE.
WE
ARE

-DR. BAK NGUYEN

Chapter 16
"The Fire of Life"
Speech by Dr. Bak Nguyen

**Life is free.
Our birth's right is liberty.
We started life with our legacy.**
- Dr. Bak Nguyen

From there, we must earn stripes and knowledge to embrace the gift of life. Easy and hard, playful, and painful, our journey will be unique. Unique because we choose the path every step of the way.

No lives are alike, and yet, so many stay diffused in the crowd. Maybe because they choose so, maybe because they didn't know, but all are.

We all bear in us the **FIRE OF LIFE**, that vital force shining through our eyes, that curiosity for more, that impatience to move. That's the **FIRE OF LIFE**.

Will we choose to feed it our passions and soul, we will keep it lilting the candle on our table. In both cases, we will have received the same gift, the same opportunity, the only difference was what and how often we chose to feed it.

Take the fire out in the open, and it will grow and be seen miles around. From the horizon, people will see the light and the promise of warmth.

From their perception, it is impossible to distinguish the bearer from the flame. We are one with the fire. We have become one with the fire.

Passion is the word, and excitement is the feeling. The **FIRE OF LIFE** can fuel many causes: **Hope**, **Audacity**, **Defiance**, **Freedom** as much as **Jealousy**, **Greed**, and **War**. Its role was not to choose but to empower what is, what is chosen.

The **FIRE OF LIFE** is a gift. Wrongly put to use, it will be the heaviest of burdens, burning our skins as a curse for life. The fire will never die, even from death, it will just go on to another heart.

The **FIRE OF LIFE** will always reveal the real face of his bearer. There is no hiding from it nor cheating it. Every single time, it will take our hearts and shine through its most profound fears and secrets as it will empower our desire for greatness.

The **FIRE OF LIFE** is the nemesis of Time, both racing each other before death comes knocking for its due. A **LionHeart**'s secret power is to **bend Time** in the **FIRE OF LIFE**.

In the process, he has forged his character from the same fire. That's how are forged the instruments of God and the vessel for the greater good.

We will have to choose what we will feed the fire with, because the heat may come from the flame, the smells and colors come from what it was feed with.

We are what we eat, so is the fire of life.
- Dr. Bak Nguyen

The **FIRE OF LIFE** is our second gift, after life itself. Like life, it comes from the divine and it is sacred. To waste it will not go unforgiven. To misuse its power will have consequences that we will bear and leave to as legacy to the next generations.

Feed the Fire and embrace Life, but always, stay humble, we are not the flame, we might stand with it, feel the magic and the heat, but **we are the bearer**, serving the divine.

As we choose to do so. Forget that, and we will have chosen to feed the Fire with our pride. The Fire with go on, and we won't survive it. Be warned, stay humble, and go on with the flame.

Citizen of the worlds, entrepreneurs, **LionHearts**, will we burn our world to the ground or energized it with passion, we are free to choose.

The **FIRE OF LIFE** will make it so, whatever we've decided. That's why we are so powerful, because we are both **freedom** and **fire**. We choose to forge, we choose to burn, we choose to light. Our legacy will tell the difference, not Life.

As a citizen of the world, we must awaken to our powers and put them to good use. Will we be loud and lead, be bold and create or kind and supportive, we choose. Our world needs all of us to prosper and thrive as a whole, as a kind.

Citizen of the world, entrepreneurs, **LionHearts**, I salute you.

—

EVERYTHING

ONCE

STARTED

LITTLE.

LITTLENESS,

NOT

SMALLNESS

-DR. BAK NGUYEN

—

Chapter 17
"We are all small-minded people."
Speech by Dr. Bak Nguyen

We are all small-minded people since the smartest among us only use 10% of their brain. Fight this as much as you want, until we've reached the next stage of evolution, that's who we are. Should we be ashamed?

On the contrary, we should be proud, and we made it this far with only 10%! We were smart enough to network between us to build on each of those single 10%. 10 plus ten plus ten plus ten. That's how we raised cities and nations.

Every 10% counts to make the difference, as it adds up and compounds with the other. We are all in it together. Believe that!

We should stand tall and proud of our little minds. We made it because we have access to **100% of our heart**. We know who we are and where we want to go.

The 10% will ease the day because 100% is leading the way.
- Dr. Bak Nguyen

That's why beliefs are bigger than knowledge. We can only know what has already been. But we can believe in what will be. Since the future is what will be, that's the **power of belief** is in the **greatness of our heart**.

100% belief, 100% will, 10% knowledge, and 110% evolution.
- Dr. Bak Nguyen

Do the math, one time, two times, three times, and the results will never be the same. It will just grow and grow.

The percentage may stay the same, but the number rapidly outgrow what our minds can compound. Should we be afraid? Only if we think that our greatness resides in our **10%'s mind**.

With 10%, what do we have to lose to open it up? With 10%, why are we so protective of what's inside? Be proud, be smart, get over it, that's just a **small mind, protected by a big pride**.

Pride has the power of a doorman, to open and shut the doors. Its holds a key role, to hold the door of our mind.

Make sure it gets the notice to keep the doors open no matter the time of the day, no matter the seasons, no matter the mood. If it cannot uphold his responsibility, fire it and let the doors unlocked. That was only 10%.

What we need to safeguard is the **purpose of Life**, the one leading the way, always the first charging in the front of the line, our **LionHearts**.

That 100% does not back down, does not doubt nor pretend. That 100% charms and charges. That 100% conquers and rallies. That 100% helps and builds. The **LionHeart** does not need protection, it needs movement and actions. Its only needs to be fed so it can, in turn, feed and inspire others.

Citizen of the world, entrepreneurs, **LionHearts**, embrace the 100% every day over that 10%. But wait, we don't need to choose, we can build with the whole 110%.

So why are we even here talking about it? Why? Because of that door's holder that so often misplaced its importance in the matter.

Citizen of the world, entrepreneurs, **LionHearts**, we may have pity, even as we are humble and generous, we must do what must be done without hesitation. The first task required of us is to keep our pride in check or simply fire it! You are fired, Pride!

We'll may have to open the door ourself, even hold the door to other, but we haven't lost anything of value. Even with 10%, we can surely look for the knob! I trust we can.

Citizen of the world, entrepreneurs, **LionHearts**, we are all small-minded people since the smartest among us only use 10% of their brand. And we are proud and thankful for it.

We have made it this far, and it was only the beginning. A bright future awaits us ahead, and through the journey, we will push the limits further, we will succeed, we might even get to 11%! The satisfaction will be 100%. I assured you.

Citizen of the world, entrepreneurs, **LionHearts**, I salute you.

THE ONLY
FORCE
WITHOUT
A SHADOW IS
OUR WILL

-DR. BAK NGUYEN

Chapter 18
"The Essence of Time"
Speech by Dr. Bak Nguyen

Time is a gift. A gift for life, a chance to leave our trail in the Universe. Time nurses us from childhood and allows us to grow into our journey.

Kind and abundant, Time then, slowly imposes its rules: its only moves forward and cannot be stopped, paused or cheated. But our perception of Time, that's a different story.

We can be audacious and successful or small and fearful, in the eye of Time, we are all the same. Some of us will have more time to spend while some will make the most of their short given time.

Actually, it's not as defined as we might think. We are born with a certain amount of vital energy. As we live, we can simply spend it and fade away as we've depleted it. That's the natural way of Life. Actually, that's the baseline.

Our kind is known to be ingenious. We've evolved from the baseline of life. We have discovered and mastered ways to harness and replenish our vitality as we live through our journey. We all do it.

Love is the most popular way known to all.

Without Love, Life is colorless and Time is a burden.
- Dr. Bak Nguyen

But once we loved and are loved in return, both vitality and time take a new meaning. We feel taller because we matter to another soul. We feel stronger because we have opened our heart. We are in love, and time feels now weightless.

Another way to harness vitality and blend Time is through **creativity**. As we explore the possibilities of our mind and soul, we have the chance to play with the same elements that God used to assemble the Universe.

We are no Gods, and we have access to a few of his perfect tools. It is through those tools that the divine will transcend in us. As we become the tool itself, just like the bearer and the **FIRE OF LIFE** with be blended, we will command Time, for a short while.

> ## To create is a privilege, a privilege to reorganize the Universe and to have access to its fabric.
> ### - Dr. Bak Nguyen

The first change of creativity is to ourself. No mind that has created will ever remain the same. The minute we've touched the fabric of the Universe, that minute, we've started to grow and evolve, at least from our perspective of things.

The vitality of creativity is an enhanced formula to Happiness and Greatness.
- Dr. Bak Nguyen

It's as magical as love. Sometimes, we even call it self-love. Those who have access to the power to create will bend Time and harness vitality as naturally as they breathe. Innocence, the openness of both the mind and heart, and the profound desire to evolve will lead the way to creativity.

There is a third way to harness vitality and escape from the grasp of Time, at least for a moment: to master the **Power of Generosity**.

Generosity is one of the most powerful ways to matter and to take our place in the Universe, to be part of it. It works differently than the power of creativity. We cannot just access the fabric of the divine to evolve. We have to rise beyond ourself and become part of the divine.

We don't have generosity, and we are generosity.
- Dr. Bak Nguyen

As we include more and more individuals to our sight, our heart will inevitably have to grow to make room for all these people. Even if they will leave eventually, the extra room we made will remain and ready to welcome newcomers.

No one with a generous heart is poor; no one with a big heart is weak. Like a gift included in the package, the generous hearts are kind, wise, and strong. They attract and shine through any darkness, through any thickness.

To them, Time is a friend as Time empowers their ability to multiply abundance. Generosity is not simply the act of giving.

Generosity is a state of mind where one is expected to provide. To provide more than to himself.

To the generous hearts, vitality never runs out. Like tequila, it will let be until it hits, in a simple knockout. The day Death comes, the generous hearts might not even notice the transition.

Be generous, and you will be limitless.
- Dr. Bak Nguyen

Citizen of the world, entrepreneurs, **LionHearts**, we are all subjected to the realm of Time. There is no escape from it, but there are ways to rise above the its grasp.

Love, **creativity**, and **generosity** are ways to master Time and make it into an ally. So love, create, and be generous. Do it for yourself, do it to feel great, do it to matter!

We've all received the gift of life, and we have access to the Universe, why starring at it wandering? Be! Reach for it, for its fabric and start to matter, to us and the Universe.

That is how worlds are made; that is how kindness is spread, that is how our heart will have the power of ten suns. Citizen of the worlds, love, create, be generous. Elevate yourself and the rest of the world with you.

Citizen of the world, entrepreneurs, lions hearts, I salute you!

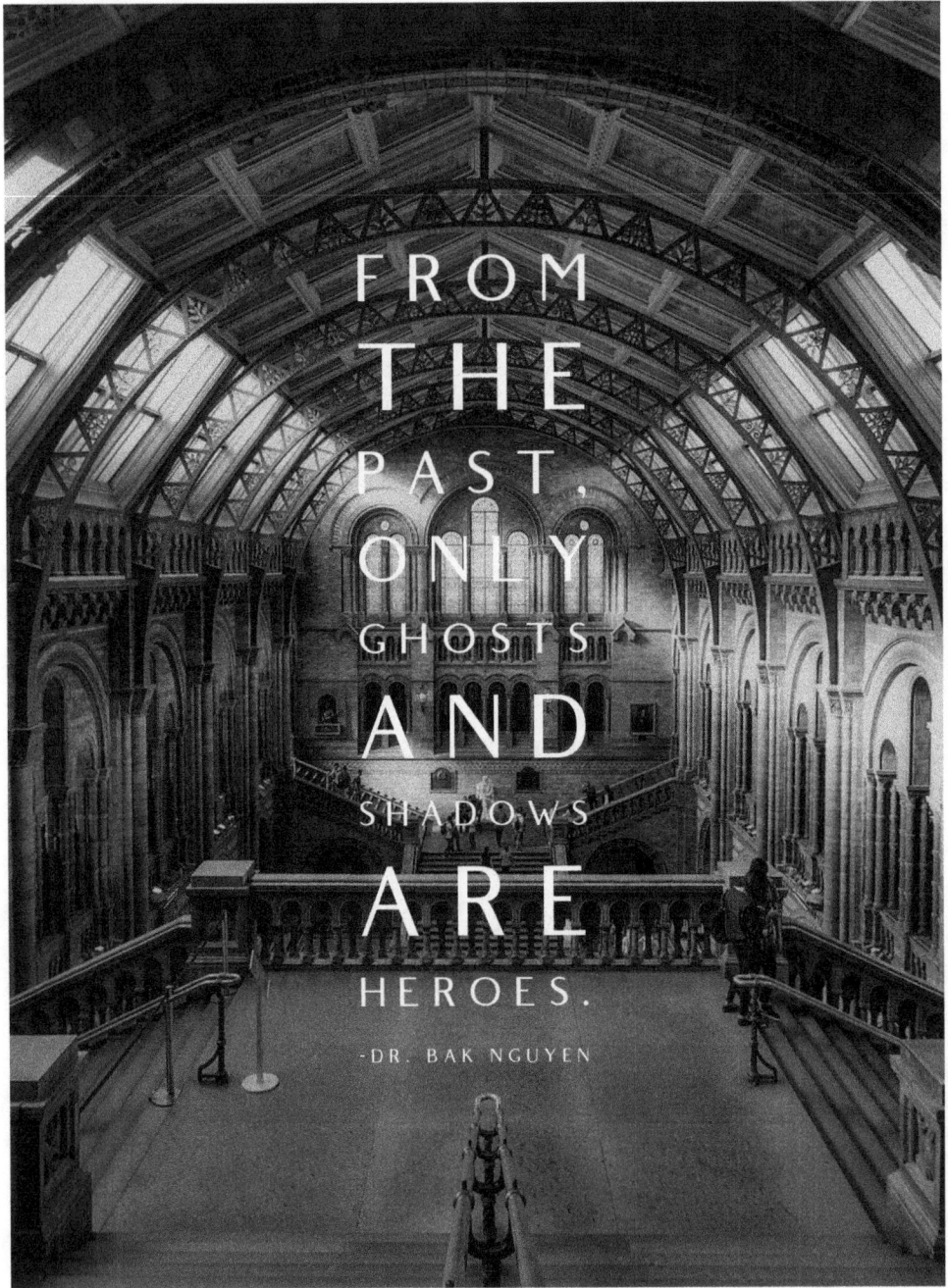

FROM THE PAST, ONLY GHOSTS AND SHADOWS ARE HEROES.

-DR. BAK NGUYEN

Chapter 19
"The Rise of the Soul"
Speech by Dr. Bak Nguyen

The **Soul of Doubt** continuously looks upon our shoulder as a shadow. Every call, every decision, Doubt make us feel small. When we let it be, Doubt likes to ridicule us and make us feel like idiots.

The strong minds among us have learned to discard it as a weakness to be ignored and erased. This would be a mistake. I can't believe that I am saying those words out loud against my own beliefs.

I will be a mistake to erase Doubt.
- Dr. Bak Nguyen

We only need to keep it in check as we do with Pride, the doorman to our mind. Not a gatekeeper, a doorman.

I don't like Doubt anymore than any of you. I hate the feelings of smallness and the second-guessing it bears within. But as I write these words, I realize that the feelings were not within doubt, they were within me.

If I feel small, it's because I am not sure. If I second guess, it's because I know, somewhere deep in my soul, that there is something else I haven't thought through.

Then I realized that Doubt is an enemy to crush while we execute, but Doubt is also that little annoying helper to our intelligence while we plan.

It makes us look a little deeper, a little wider, a little differently. That's its role, that how it should remain, little. Do not take the pleasure to feed your doubts as you feed your heart. It's a path of hard, very hard return.

A strong heart is not afraid of doubt. A **LionHeart** is so big that Doubt will never bear enough influence to corrupt its Will.

Feed your heart, not your doubts.
- Dr. Bak Nguyen

Believe, believe to rise above fear and pride. Believe to accept that we are human, nothing more. Being human is among the best chance that we have!

We have received the **gift of Life**, so have all living creatures. Then, we've received the **gift of Freedom** and the **gift of Creativity**. That's much power given to one soul. With each gift, comes its shadow, not as a price to pay or a poisoned apple, it's just the way of the universe is.

To each force, it is a nemesis to keep the balance. From the reaction between the opposites derives the energy of the universe, we call it vitality.
- Dr. Bak Nguyen

The **shadow of Creativity** is **Pride**. On one hand, we've touched the divine and started to play with the fabric of the Universe. It is intoxicating as it can bend the existence of Time itself.

If we don't know who we are and our purpose in this world, we will get lost and think that we are gods. If we fail that test, we will have lost the only battle that we might never come back from, the battle against our personal evil, our Pride.

In all the legends, the best sword against a hero is it's own. Don't fall under yours, your Pride.
- Dr. Bak Nguyen

Handsome and tall, Pride is nothing more than the doorman to our mind. If we know that we have to keep the doors of our mind opened at all time, we don't need a doorman! We just need a door holder! Why the waste of energy?

To rise beyond, Pride has to grow beyond oneself. What we've created can either be at our level or, if we are humble enough to believe that we were just a tool, what we've created will not be limited to our vision.

We will give it our best, and it will have a life on its own. That's when the growth becomes exponential. Have we planned for it? Do we even know how to count this far? It does not matter, and we were wise enough to give it our best and let it be.

With Humility, we will make the most of the gift of Creativity without the shadow of pride.
- Dr. Bak Nguyen

The **shadow of Freedom** is **Fear**. Yes, we can. So we will. We will walk, we will fall, we will do, mistakes and greatnesses, we will. Every time, we will have to keep our heart in check because there will be no one to blame, successes, and failures. It was our free will.

Free and Will. We have. We are.
- Dr. Bak Nguyen

So yes, we can choose to rise. To raise with honor, to believe in ourself and in our part to play in the Universe or we can choose to embrace Doubt and Fear, and look down at the edge instead of looking up. We choose.

If you think of it, Fear is what makes Freedom so great. We knew there was fear and we rose above it. That's personal greatness. As **Humility** with keeping our **Pride** in check, to keep Fear in check, we need the power of the heart, the **power of Generosity**.

As long as I know that our powers are intended to help others, to serve in the greater whole, and to matter, Fear has no bearing.

The only force without a shadow is our Will.
- Dr. Bak Nguyen

Citizen of the world, entrepreneurs, **LionHearts**, believe in yourself, believe that you are good, that you will succeed Believe that together, we will make God proud!

Will is not a gift that we've received. Will is what we've forged, from the **Fire of Life**. Will is our signature in the Universe, the key to our role in the whole.

The strength of your Will will dictate the world we are living in.
- Dr. Bak Nguyen

Citizen of the world, entrepreneurs, **LionHearts**, we are all in it together. We have to forge our Will every day. We have to enforce our Will at every turn. Our Will is what has pushed us this far. That's a success, that's a win, that's the difference: the Will we have forged.

Feed your Will and your heart, not your doubts. Believe and embrace, be generous and stand tall, because we are what we believe, we have what we've received, **Free and Will**.

Be generous, be grateful, put your powers to good use, and build greatness and kindness. Citizen of the world, entrepreneurs, **LionHearts**, there are no ones to blame but ourselves. There are no ones to build but ourselves. The fate of our world rests upon our shoulders.

Citizen of the world, entrepreneurs, **LionHearts**, I salute you.

DON'T SPEND

TOO MUCH TIME

LOOKING FOR YOUR NAME.

SPEND TIME

FORGING YOUR

NAME IN THE

FIRE OF LIFE.

-DR. BAK NGUYEN

Chapter 20
"The Lies of Sacrifice"
Speech by Dr. Bak Nguyen

Sacrifices, we have to let go to make it. We have to give up today in order to have more tomorrow. That's what we are told. That's a lie.

A sacrifice is not an investment. A sacrifice is a statement, a choice. Be aware, be warned. Some will lie to our face to take advantage of us.

Others, with very good intentions to help, will repeat the **lies of sacrifice** because they believe truly believe that it was the only way to make it through. They were honest, there were also corrupted from the essence of Life.

The worst part of the lie is that they will be proven right, with sacrifices, we will get ahead. Painfully and slowly, they will walk forward with the self-imposed scars on their heart.

Sacrifices will reinforce Will, but it will also corrupt the soul with melancholy and a bitter taste, not from Life but from the lies.
- Dr. Bak Nguyen

They are another ways. We talked about sacrifice because we chose to divide and subtract instead of embrace creativity and abundance to add up and multiply.

Both ways are actions taken, are Will set in motion. The journey has begun, there is no return from it. We will keep moving. We will grow. But why the bitter taste?

Worst, we will think that bitter is part of Life! It is not true! We choose bitterness and division while we could have chosen abundance and generosity.

Sacrifices do not always embody generosity and nobility.
- Dr. Bak Nguyen

We choose to reduce our minds and hearts to the small instead of to be humble enough to accept our littleness in the Universe and to ask for reinforcements.

Sacrifice is the pride of thinking that we, alone, can be the difference. Yes, we can make a difference, as a part of a whole, but we are not the whole by ourselves. No one can ever be the whole by themselves!

One is no whole, one is not unity.
- Dr. Bak Nguyen

What about half of one?! That's the lie of sacrifices. We are little in the whole. Being little has nothing to do with being small.

Being small is to reduce the entry to our mind and heart. Being little is to know and be wise enough, to have the humility to accept what we are part in the vastness of the canvas, the whole.

Don't get me wrong, sacrifices are hard, hard choices. It is pain, condensed. Sacrifice shows character and strength. But also taint everything darker.

Remember why we are. We are here to look for happiness. That's true gift of **Life**, of **Abundance**, of **Creativity**. Add up and multiple, include, and share.

Sacrifices are not about giving,

It is about proving a point.

Sharing is about giving.

Abundance is about giving.

Heroes come in many sizes and shapes, as are **LionHearts**. They can be rich or poor, it all depends on the choices they made: to divide or to multiple, to subtract or to add up.

How can we be part of the whole if we have a tendency to divide and subtract? If we do, we will make the Universe smaller, not greater.

The Universe is always expanding, so should our minds and hearts.
- Dr. Bak Nguyen

So why don't we show the same love and kindness to ourselves, to embrace the endless possibilities of abundance, to create while we add up and multiple? That's the natural course of the divine.

Look at any learning child, adding up comes naturally to them. Teach them to subtract, and you will see their whole body rejecting the corrupted code.

Be generous and kind enough to spare them the unnecessary pain and lie. Be kind to yourself and leave that lie behind.

Citizen of the world, entrepreneurs, **LionHearts**, we don't need to be more tested than our journey requires. We don't need armors nor scars that won't make us grow naturally.

To divide is not.

To suffer is not always necessary.

To be strong is not something to play with.

We are not strong because we want to prove and make a point. We are strong when we serve others and take our place in the Universe, part of the whole.

The formula is to include and add up, the Universe will multiply it exponentially. Give in and trust in Abundance, in Positivity, in Kindness, in Generosity.

We won't have to suffer, to doubt, to overthink nor to fear, because our heart will have outgrown the animal's condition, maybe even the human's condition. We will have embraced happiness and grown into the whole.

Citizen of the world, entrepreneurs, **LionHearts**, we are all in it together, as a whole. A whole Universe, a whole world, a whole soul, a whole body.

To divide is not divine.
To subtract is not natural.
- Dr. Bak Nguyen

What we feed our minds and hearts will paint how we see the world. Why the pain? The purpose of power is to serve. The purpose of intelligence is to ease the way. The purpose of love is to have access to the whole.

The Universe is kind and abundant. Our world can be kind and abundant. I know that my world will be. How about yours? Free and Will, we have, we are.

Citizen of the world, entrepreneurs, **LionHearts**, make your choice. Citizen of the world, entrepreneurs, **LionHearts**, I salute you!

LEAVE,

LIVE AND LEAD.

-DR. BAK NGUYEN

Chapter 21
"Compounded Wills"
Speech by Dr. Bak Nguyen

Living life is a privilege. Thriving in this life is a choice. A choice that only we can make. We will all be looking for happiness, to find back that natural state of mind we tasted in our childhood.

It was a birthright and we will earn it back! We can choose to play it safe. But safe is average. The known is average. It might have been great yesterday, today it's average.

That's why we cannot get attached to anything, neither to the past nor to our previous achievements. They are now part of the average. No new greatness will emerge from the past nor the average.

As wise as it is possible to forgive one's mistake, it also can be rewarding to forget that event. To move on and to leave it behind. As we should do, to move forward and be ready to jump headfirst again.

Our past successes are only legends and stories meant to be told as we finish our evenings around a fire. Nothing more.

From the past, only ghosts and shadows are heroes.
- Dr. Bak Nguyen

It is just not possible that the shadow stands in front of us if we are looking at the sun. So face the sun, and the shadow will always stay behind, with the past and the average.

Ancient wisdom taught us to move forward, to not look back, no matter what we've left behind. Fail to do so, and we will turn into those statues of salt.

At the first raindrop, what's left of us will simply meltdown and fade away. The image is vivid, and the essence is pure truth. The greatness awaits again, forward, in the future.

Citizen of the world, entrepreneurs, **LionHearts**, move on and leave the past and the average behind.

Leave, live, and lead!
- Dr. Bak Nguyen

The work and sweat we put in have contributed to raise the average. We raised it, pulling it with the strength of our Will. Our shoulders stabilized the rise when we were still looking a for strong footing as we gave it our best!

We must move on. We gave, now we move. We did, now we must be. We were, now we are looking for more!

We are not average. We will not forget who we are and be swallowed by the average. We refuse to stay and to be consumed by the past.

Citizen of the world, entrepreneurs, **LionHearts**, the world needs us to stay hungry, to stay thirsty for more growth. That's Life, life to the fullest, a life worth living, a life that will echo and matter to others.

Life is about being happy. That's a promise, a goal. It is there, and it is near, it is within us to make it happen. We can choose to create unlimited abundance in our life.

The more, the better. Because the more we have, the more we will give. The more we will give, the more we will grow. And we will grow even bigger as we learn to leave it all behind, taking ahead only the insurance that we can give even more!

More! Not less. Life is about being positive. We add up, and nature will multiple, exponentially. We chose that team, and we embraced the idea. So that's what will be.

The result is our **compounded Wills** adding up to achieve greatness. The Universe is expanding, thus will we if we tune in to its frequency.

Our hearts can beat at its pace if we stay sensitive, humble. Our minds can vibrate with its chords if we stay open and ready. Not just for a moment, but at any given time.

The only way to get to the future is to have the sails always ready to harness the winds and to surf the tides. Life is an adventure, make yours exciting!

**Life can be about us if we make it
about others first.**
- Dr. Bak Nguyen

If we are honest, really honest, everything we do comes down to us. So what? If goodness, generosity, wisdom, greatness derived for the littleness of one's self?

I would love to meet that littleness because it is a **LionHeart** beating, because of it a legend in writing, because it is life inspiring.

**Everything once started little.
Littleness, not smallness.**
- Dr. Bak Nguyen

From littleness, we can build and grow. Littleness was simply a starting point, a fact in time. It will not stay little for long, but it will be little, always, in perspective with the whole.

Littleness can be great. Littleness can move mountains because it stay open to the possibility, and made it into an opportunity. Littleness is openness.

Do not confuse littleness and smallness. One is a status in time while the other is a chosen state of mind.

We were born little, but some will choose to stay small. That's not the same.
- Dr. Bak Nguyen

To grow, we must add up, multiple. To multiple, we must share. To share, we must give and give. To gain speed, we must give more, faster, better, and we must grow to inspire.

To inspire more **LionHearts**, to launch and support the eagles, to empower the citizens of the world. We are all in this together, as a whole. So let grow our team!

A team assembled to achieve greatness, a team that will make the most out of each day thanks to the compounded Wills of each of its member.

Compounded Wills, not averaged Wills.
- Dr. Bak Nguyen

Because a Will will inspire another one to surpass itself, to beat his/her last win. And from the next win, we will build more, bigger, taller, kinder.

The last win, the past win, is simply a stepping stone, not a cornerstone.
- Dr. Bak Nguyen

That's the team, that's our team. A team that sleeps with hopes and dreams, a team that embraces the challenge with audacity and passion. Our team will win; there is no other way; we will win!

That's what we believe, that's who we are, citizen of the worlds, entrepreneurs, and **LionHearts**. Remember, we are all in this together, as a whole.

Victory will be ours, and Happiness will be shared, our world will shine!

Citizen of the world, entrepreneurs, **LionHearts**, I salute you!

THE VITALITY

OF CREATIVITY

IS AN

ENHANCED

FORMULA

TO HAPPINESS

AND GREATNESS

-DR. BAK NGUYEN

CONCLUSION
"The Train of Life"
Speech by Dr. Bak Nguyen

Life is a race. Sure. Life is a journey. Life is what greets us every morning as long as we are willing to wake up and embrace the day.

Will today brings joy and victory or bear challenges and tests? The choice is ours to make. Always. Life is fulfilling and beautiful if we see the opportunity and face the light of hope, leaving the shadow of doubt behind us. It's pure physics, and it works every single time. So what will your day bring to our world?

To keep advancing, push through the journey. We need to know what we want. For that to happen, we need to know who we are, really are, deep down. It is only when we've embraced ourselves completely, as part of the whole, that we can start to walk our true journey, to start drafting our legend.

The **Quest of Identity** was only the entrance to the canvas of Life. We need to rise in control to start writing our destiny.

Don't spend too much of your life looking for a name. Spend time forging your name in the fire of life.
- Dr. Bak Nguyen

We are all in this, together, as a whole. Each of us counts as part of the team. We can bear more on our shoulders or look at the others pulling their weight, only us will decide of our role in the Universe.

As soon as we've carried more than our own weight, we've made a difference. And then, we will notice that it wasn't that hard. We will want to do more, to pull more and before we even notice, we've changed, we've grown.

Life can be lonely. Our **Quest of Identity** surely was. But the journey of Life is a much greater quest. It doesn't have to be lonely.

Choose your values and embrace your Destiny. From the path, true Loyalty will keep us company. We are all in this together, as a whole.

It is only as a whole that we start to grow into greatness.
- Dr. Bak Nguyen

We don't need to fight among ourselves for the carrots anymore. We can choose to stand tall, together, as a whole, go for the elephants, and reach for the stars. Life is abundant if we choose to look beyond the horizon instead of looking at our feet.

We don't need to be carrots eater forever. We have the freedom to choose for ourselves. And no one will do it for us. Stay hesitant and be warned that we just chose to stay behind. Nobody has chosen in your place even if we thought otherwise.

Open your heart and your mind to yourself and to Life! Our world will be stronger with each one of us embracing our freedom and make something out of our compounded Wills! Together, as a whole! We are citizens of the world!

To keep marching in the right direction, we will need help. The smell of Death do just that. It will be that friend. It will keep us on our toes and challenge us to dares, beyond our imagination.

Our greatest win will come the day we'll look it in the eyes, and there will be no regrets left for it to feed on! We will kiss death, but not yet!

Until then, Time will keep us company to remind us that life is happening now, moving forward, always. It's a law of nature. But there are ways to bend the rules, to bend Time itself.

The power lies in each of our heart. The power of Generosity. The power of love! Like Death, Time is an ally, caring for as long as we face the light of Hope and are moving forward!

To love is to respect one's right to find out more of oneself. To care is to be there when one's require an open heart to share with.
- Dr. Bak Nguyen

A generous heart will never go hungry or deprived. It will stay hungry, but never out of resources. Safe is part of the past. Nothing great will comes from the known. Yesterday, it might have been great. Today, it's the new average.

Knowing that the smartest among us only use 10% of their brain, why make such a big deal out of it? The power is in the heart. That's where vibes the Universe.

For as long as our hearts lead the day, our mind and intelligence will ease the way.
- Dr. Bak Nguyen

Our hearts are the only ones that can stir through the tides of Greed and Fear and keep us on the track. It's simple, natural. Our heart just needs to beat, consistent, strong, at its own pace until it is ready to grow into Momentum.

Don't stand in the way of a loyal heart because it is no victory possible.
- Dr. Bak Nguyen

Stay humble, and we will avoid the falls on the road. Remember that to grow, and we need to feed, every day, new tastes, new colors, unique shapes.

We are what we eat. If we eat the same again and again, we will stay the same, left behind by the train of Life.

So why do we need a doorman to our minds and hearts? Pride is just a doorman that needs to keep the doors opened at all time and welcome Life in. Pride is a door holder, not a gatekeeper! Don't waste more time and energy on it.

And the rewards are great, trust me! A mind growing is the key to Abundance. Its creativity will ease our way, every single time.

We only need to allow it to be, and to trust in ourselves. An open heart grows and, even with the scars adding up, it becomes stronger at each beat. If we keep growing, we will grow into our Destiny, the legend of the **LionHeart**.

We were all born little, but some will choose to stay small. That's not the same.
- Dr. Bak Nguyen

Keep your Pride in check, and you'll be just fine. It's not that hard, we only need to choose. We choose. Even with only 10%, we are ingenious, and have made it this far! Because we were smart enough to build on everyone's 10%. That was the How.

The real greatness comes from the What. With a nation of hearts beating as one, we will achieve greatness with our Wills. Our Will to make the day, to make the difference, to matter.

To matter, we have to serve. To serve not ourselves, but the others. The legend is not about the goal, but the journey. That's about us, our journey.

To march forward and matter, we need leaders, **LionHearts** who will show the way, open the march, and inspire others to join the march of Life, and eventually, lead themselves one day.

Some of us are meant to be lions, others are eagles and others are trees. The strength of the lions is their heart. The power of the eagles is their minds and vision. The force of the trees is the unity of the forest. The whole is taking its vitality from the powers of each kind, from every single one of our hearts. Lions, eagles or trees, our world needs you. It needs all of you!

Citizen of the world, entrepreneurs, **LionHearts**, know who you are and be great, together! That's true leadership, the only leadership that matters. The knowledge to know oneself and master our destiny as part of a greater whole!

Feed yourself every day with new things, the right values. We are what we eat. We are all citizens of the world!

Our world is not black and white nor good or bad. We made sure of that, by adapting. We can honor the past and build upon it. We can do better, and build upon the hopes of the past generations. We are all in this together!

Citizen of the world, entrepreneurs, **LionHearts**, be smart, be strong, be generous, be flexible, be kind. Master your heart, that's true leadership! Are you ready for greatness?

Citizen of the world, entrepreneurs, **LionHearts**, I salute you!

EAX

TOTAL
IMMERSION WITH
ENHANCED AUDIO EXPERIENCE

Streaming Audiobook Blockbuster

Search for Dr. Bak Nguyen on SPOTIFY, Apple Music
and all major music platforms

EAX

ENHANCED AUDIO EXPERIENCE

A new way to learn and enjoy Audiobooks. Made to be entertaining while keeping the self-educational value of a book, EAX will appeal to both auditive and visual people. EAX is the blockbuster of the Audiobooks.

EAX will cover most of Dr. Bak's books, and is now negotiating to bring more authors and more titles to the EAX concept.

Now streaming on Spotify, Apple Music and available for download on all major music platforms. Give it a try today!

FROM THE SAME AUTHOR
Dr. Bak Nguyen

www.DrBakNguyen.com

BUSINESS

La Symphonie des Sens
ENTREPREUNARIAT
par DR BAK NGUYEN

Industries Disruptors
BY DR. BAK NGUYEN, ROUBA SAKR AND COLLABORATORS

Changing the World from a dental chair
BY DR. BAK NGUYEN

The Power Behind the Alpha
BY TRANIE VO & DR. BAK NGUYEN

SELFMADE
GRATITUDE AND HUMILITY
BY DR. BAK NGUYEN

CHAMPION MINDSET
LEARNING TO WIN

BY DR. BAK NGUYEN & CHRISTOPHE MULUMBA

FACTEUR HUMAIN
LE LEADERSHIP DU SUCCÈS
par DR BAK NGUYEN & CHRISTIAN TRUDEAU

ehappyPedia
THE RISE OF THE UNICORN
BY DR. BAK NGUYEN & DR. JEAN DE SERRES

BRANDING DR.BAK
BALANCING STRATEGY AND EMOTIONS
BY DR. BAK NGUYEN, BRENDA GARCIA & SANTIAGO CHICA

CHILDREN'S BOOK
with William Bak

The Trilogy of Legends

THE LEGEND OF THE CHICKEN HEART
BY DR. BAK NGUYEN & WILLIAM BAK

THE LEGEND OF THE LION HEART
BY DR. BAK NGUYEN & WILLIAM BAK

THE LEGEND OF THE DRAGON HEART
BY DR. BAK NGUYEN & WILLIAM BAK

WE ARE ALL DRAGONS
BY DR. BAK NGUYEN & WILLIAM BAK

HOW TO WRITE A BOOK IN 30 DAYS
BY DR. BAK NGUYEN

POWER
EMOTIONAL INTELLIGENCE
BY DR. BAK NGUYEN

MENTORS
BY DR. BAK NGUYEN

HOW TO NOT FAIL AS A DENTIST
BY DR. BAK NGUYEN

HOW TO WRITE A SUCCESSFUL BUSINESS PLAN
BY DR. BAK NGUYEN & ROUBA SAKR

MINDSET ARMORY
BY DR. BAK NGUYEN

PARENTING

THE BOOK OF LEGENDS
BY DR. BAK NGUYEN & WILLIAM BAK

THE BOOK OF LEGENDS 2
BY DR. BAK NGUYEN & WILLIAM BAK

SEFL HELP

PROFESSION HEALTH
THE UNCONVENTIONAL QUEST OF HAPPINESS
BY DR. BAK NGUYEN, DR. MIRJANA SINDOLIC,
DR. ROBERT DURAND AND COLLABORATORS

WHITE COATS
THE UNCONVENTIONAL QUEST OF HAPPINESS
BY DR. BAK NGUYEN AND COLLABORATORS

REBOOT
MIDLIFE CRISIS
BY DR. BAK NGUYEN

HUMILITY FOR SUCCESS
IT'S REALLY NOT WHAT YOU THINK
BY DR. BAK NGUYEN

PHILOSOPHY

IDENTITY
THE ANTHOLOGY OF QUESTS
BY DR. BAK NGUYEN

HYBRID
THE MODERN QUEST OF IDENTITY
BY DR. BAK NGUYEN

FORCES OF NATURE
FORGING THE CHARACTER OF WINNERS
BY DR. BAK NGUYEN

SOCIETY

LEADERSHIP
PANDORA'S BOX
BY DR. BAK NGUYEN

KRYPTO
TO SAVE THE WORLD
BY DR. BAK NGUYEN & ILYAS BAKOUCH

LE RÊVE CANADIEN
D'IMMIGRANT À MILLIONNAIRE
par DR BAK NGUYEN

LIFESTYLE - TRAVEL - MINDSET

HORIZON, BUILDING UP THE VISION
VOLUME ONE
BY DR. BAK NGUYEN

HORIZON, ON THE FOOTSTEP OF TITANS

VOLUME TWO
BY DR. BAK NGUYEN

www.DrBakNguyen.com

DR.

Bnk Nguyen